INVOKE THE GODS

Exploring the Power of Male Archetypes

WHY INVOKE A GOD?

Wouldn't it be easier to go straight to the top, and petition the Cosmic Intelligence rather than a demi-god?

Demi-gods are like finely tuned instruments honed to a particular task. Working through them intensifies and refines our intent. It has long been recognized that concentrating on a specific godform elicits a particular response. Gods arise in answer to the everchanging needs of the populace; there is one for every possible situation. In homing in on the symbols, personality, history, and seasonal referents of an individual deity, we activate a link both on a conscious and subconscious level, and find the qualities represented by the archetype infinitely more accessible.

—Kala Trobe

About the Author

Kala Trobe (England) holds an Honors degree in English Literature and manages an antiquarian bookshop in England. She has traveled extensively and visited many of the world's sacred sites. Her experience includes working as a professional Tarot reader, medium, and vocational healer.

To Write to the Author

If you wish to contact the author or would like more information about this book, please write to the author in care of Llewellyn Worldwide and we will forward your request. Both the author and publisher appreciate hearing from you and learning of your enjoyment of this book and how it has helped you. Llewellyn Worldwide cannot guarantee that every letter written to the author can be answered, but all will be forwarded. Please write to:

Kala Trobe
℅ Llewellyn Worldwide
P.O. Box 64383, Dept. 0-7387-0096-7
St. Paul, MN 55164-0383, U.S.A.

Please enclose a self-addressed stamped envelope for reply, or $1.00 to cover costs. If outside U.S.A., enclose international postal reply coupon.

Many of Llewellyn's authors have websites with additional information and resources. For more information, please visit our website at:

http://www.llewellyn.com

INVOKE

Exploring the Power of

THE

Male Archetypes

GODS

KALA TROBE

2001

Llewellyn Publications

St. Paul, Minnesota 55164-0383, U.S.A.

First Edition
First Printing, 2001

Book design: Karin Simoneau
Cover art: © 2001 Kris Waldherr
Cover design: Lisa Novak
Interior art: Kate Thomssen
Project management: Michael Maupin

Library of Congress Cataloging-in-Publication Data
Trobe, Kala, 1969–
    Invoke the gods : exploring the power of male archetypes / Kala Trobe. — 1st ed.
       p. cm.
    Includes bibliographical references (p.   ) and index.
    ISBN 0-7387-0096-7
    1. Magic. 2. Gods—Miscellanea. 3. Invocation—Miscellanea. I. Title.
  BF1623 .T76 2001
  291.2'113—dc21   2001046293

Llewellyn Publications
A Division of Llewellyn Worldwide, Ltd.
P.O. Box 64383, Dept. 0-7387-0096-7
St. Paul, MN 55164-0383, U.S.A.
www.llewellyn.com

Printed in the United States of America

OTHER BOOKS BY KALA TROBE

Invoke the Goddess

Magic of Qabalah

For Sean Groth, Dr. Mike of New Orleans,
Josef Donovan of Leigh-on-Sea,
Richard Moore, David La Trobe-Bateman,
and the other gods in my life, with love and thanks.

CONTENTS

INTRODUCTION

Invoke the Gods is a natural sequel to *Invoke the Goddess* (Llewellyn, 2000). It also came about in response to the enthusiasm some of my male friends had for the idea. They claimed that a book entirely dedicated to male deities would be a blessing indeed in the goddess-orientated field of magick.

I realize that it is unorthodox to mix reasonably in-depth analyses of mythology and literary history (particularly relevant to the Greek section) with "personal encounters," and with Tarot card references, but in this I am following in the footsteps of the Western Mystery Tradition. That these interpretations differ from those of the original worshippers of Hindu, Egyptian, and Greek deities, there is no doubt. The descriptions are based on as much empirical information as possible, but the exercises and correspondences are interpretative.

The visualizations may be experienced while reading, or performed more ritualistically, preferably with one person reading them to another, or on tape. However, just as scenes of a novel present themselves to the mind's eye, the visualizations should be easy to "experience" simply through reading.

There are some gods and goddesses whose functions are similar. Isis, for example, can help augment magickal abilities, as can Thoth. Siva, as god of yogis, might increase *Siddhi* powers to the same ends. However, their individual wavelengths are quite different, and the practitioner will naturally feel an affiliation to a particular aspect of the Cosmic Intelligence.

Some men may prefer to work with male deities, simply because they relate to them better. Some women might enjoy the polarity of working with a male god. As with all things in this dualistic world, it is a question of balance.

All of the gods and goddesses are different aspects of the one God. Like rays of different colored light through a spectrum, each wavelength has its own characteristics and properties. The greater the choice of rays, the easier to select the right one for the purpose at hand. The gods are rather like lasers, each honed to a specific set of functions.

Invoke the Gods, like *Invoke the Goddess*, aims to offer focused workings for specific ends. The key to this focus is a fund of diverse knowledge, so that the right god or goddess form might be selected. I have chosen this initial selection in parallel to the goddesses of its twin book—from Hindu, Egyptian, and Greek mythologies. Obviously there is scope for an ever-widening array of alternatives from all cultures, both male and female. Eclecticism is one of the greatest strengths of the modern witch or practitioner of magick. However, this must be coupled with accurate information and the ability to assimilate it on a personal, interactive level. This is what I hope the reader will achieve from the *Invoke* series.

INDEX TO GOD FUNCTIONS

Purpose	God
Asceticism	Siva
Athleticism	Apollo
Beauty	Krishna
Beginning, new	Khephri
Bullying, counteracting	Horus
Business	Ganesh
Career	Ganesh
Catharsis	Dionysus
Craftiness	Hermes, Hanuman
Divination	Thoth
Fidelity	Anubis
Higher purpose	Brahma
Lateral thinking	Hermes
Leadership skills	Hanuman
Love	Krishna
Magickal mysteries	Thoth
Negativity, counteracting	Ganesh
Neuroses, counteracting	Pan, Dionysus
Opposition, counteracting	Horus, Ganesh, Zeus
Perspective	Brahma

Purpose	God
Pleasure	Dionysus
Power	Zeus
Precision	Apollo
Protection	Khephri
Regeneration	Khephri
Self-control	Siva
Speech	Ra
Spellcraft	Thoth, Ra
Spirituality	Krishna, Brahma, Siva, Thoth
Status	Zeus
Strength	Zeus, Horus, Hanuman
Success in a tricky venture	Hanuman, Hermes, Ganesh
Temptation, avoiding	Siva

HINDU GODS

KRISHNA

The soft-skinned youth stood in the middle of the sword-bristling battle-ground, and spoke. His voice was pure and mellifluous, soothing the senses of the tensed troops; then it was like thunder hungry for human blood, and all who heard him found themselves confounded, except for Royal Arjuna.

"The eternal man cannot kill. The eternal man cannot die. The soul of man is not born, nor does it die. Weapons cannot cut it, fire cannot burn it; the substance of the soul is everlasting.

"Selfishness binds its host to the wheel of pain. Disinterested love and devotion liberate their practitioner from the cycle of duality. Then is sanctuary found in the gods, who create, and sustain, and destroy as they wish, but whose compassion for mankind is limitless.

"Hear me, Arjuna, and be not afraid. The friends you see on this battlefield cannot be slain by your sword, nor by any other means. They stand at the Gate between Worlds, the visible and invisible; your sword is their key, and their blood your own, for it is ordained that you should fight, Warrior, dispatching these brothers to the next stage of their progress, just as Siva himself destroys the illusion of life.

"Breathe God, be God. God flows through us, Arjuna, he fills our souls with light and fortifies this spiritual armor, which may never be pierced or removed, for it encapsulates the eternal. Our actions bespeak God, and though to nurture a moral conscience is correct, your procrastination ill befits you.

"Faith, Arjuna."

In distant bower, flanked by peacocks, I heard a cowherd sing a similar refrain.

"Faith, Radha, who clings to my knees and grinds the hem of my garments in her pale hands even as I try to quit the copse. Aeons have we spent in lovemaking, in blissful union with one another and with God, but creation is limited in its support of statis. I must move on, soon to return if you willingly release me.

"Whatever you do, dedicate it to me. In this way will all of your actions become sacrosanct. Before you eat, think of me, and in this way will your food become true nourishment. Before you work, pray to me, that I might bless your endeavor and make it fruitful in Love, the only Karma worth working for. Before you sleep, meditate on me, that I may take you one day to live in Krishnaloka, where all is beauty and abundance, and gurus of the highest integrity wait to instruct you.

"Strive, and do so in my name. When you doubt, when you are racked on the wheel of suffering, when Maya threatens to engulf your senses, speak to me. I am your friend, your guardian and your lover. I will not forsake you.

"I know what it is to live on your dense earth, to be torn by dualities, to be driven hither and thither by the wild horses of sense distraction. With devotion to God you may tame them, with love of me you may transcend the barbs of flesh-encapsulation and rise released to the loving embrace of the Celestial.

"By chanting my name and the holy name of Rama you will free yourself of the shackles of the Kali Yuga."

Krishna is an avatar of Vishnu, that is, one of the Hindu god Vishnu's many incarnations. He is a familiar godform in the West, thanks mainly to the work of A. C. Bhaktivedanta Swami Prabhupada and his followers. For decades, the Krishna Consciousness movement has spread enlightenment in the form of the Bhagavad-Gita and other writings, promoting vegetarianism, clean living, and devotion to God. The most familiar feature of the group is the joyful chanting, dancing and rhythmic percussion that accompany their many incongruous jaunts through urban centers, providing a reminder, in the midst of daily humdrum, of something far more important than shopping, working, or meeting up with friends. The Krishna devotees, with their shaved heads, *Ajna* chakra markings (above the bridge of the nose), and flowing robes, remind us of the fickle nature of transitory pleasures, of the body's impermanence, and of the pressing need to get in touch with our true spiritual source. We will each have our own technique of doing so, of course. Strict ascetic living—except when dancing up and down the street—is not everybody's method, but we all benefit from the work of any who are wholly devoted to spiritual progression.

The liberating mantra of the current age, the *Kali Yuga*, is the same as chanted perpetually by our Krishna-devoted friends. This mantra is purported to lighten the weight of *Maya*, which keeps us in earth-bound misery, and to bring our souls closer to Godhead. In this materialistic era—in Hindu chronology, the most degenerate to date—we can benefit from a perspective-gaining chant. The continual repetition of *Hare*

Krishna, Hare Krishna, Krishna Krishna Hare Hare, Hare Rama Hare Rama, Rama Rama Hare Hare, brings great spiritual insight and a profound sense of release from trivial concerns and emotional ties. It is an absolute godsend in times of emotional crisis, stilling the mind and allowing a little celestial healing to take effect. This chant, the *Maha Mantra*, translates simply as "Hail, My Lord Rama! My Lord Krishna!" Its point is to establish contact with our Cosmic Overseer, by whatever name we might identify the Mother/Father God.

Rama is another incarnation of Vishnu. The *Ramayana* epic describes the many adventures of this avatar, the major theme being that of the preservation of *Dharma*, or Universal Righteousness. Dharma is essentially the same principle as *Maat* in Egyptian lore; even the gods must obey this ethical code. There appears to be no parallel morality in Greek sacred teachings, in which gods are infallible by birthright and mortals are pawn-like "wretches." As with most embodiments of the Divine in the more compassionate religions, the purpose of Vishnu's numerous lives on earth is to bring enlightenment and salvation to mankind.

According to legend, Krishna was born in Mathura, located between Delhi and Agra. Some accounts ally his myth with the heroic escapades of a clan leader, warrior, and Krishna-cult zealot who lived in Dwaraka in around 400 B.C.E., which shows that Krishna was becoming popular at this point. He is a young godform by Indian standards, representing a new principle of love and devotion entering the Hindu religion, replacing the fear and detachment felt toward more primitive deities such as Indra.

As in the myths of Zeus with "Cronos of the crooked ways," and Jesus with the malign King Herod, it had been predicted that a boy soon to be born would overthrow the ruler (possibly indicating the influence of Asiatic religions on later Grecian and Middle Eastern mythologies), and Krishna's mother, Princess Devaki, was kept in close confines during her pregnancies. Kamsa, the king at the time of Krishna's birth, represents the old gods, eminently Indra, waiting to destroy any threat to his rule.

Unfortunately for Princess Devaki, the prophecy had specifically mentioned her eighth child. Most of the issue of the imprisoned princess had been killed at birth, but as Krishna drew his first breath, the guards fell miraculously asleep, and his father Vasudeva was able to slip from the parental confines with the baby in his arms. Then Krishna's father performed the Moses-like feat of crossing the river Yamuna, which was then in spate. As in the Biblical tale, the waters parted for him, and he crossed safely with the newly born avatar in his arms.

In Gokul, he exchanged Krishna for the daughter of a cowherd, believing that King Kamsa would balk at killing a baby girl, who could be no possible threat to him. He was wrong, and the king attempted to slay the babe he believed to be Devaki's eighth child. In true Hindi action-packed epic style, she escaped his grip and levitated skyward. Meanwhile Krishna was left to be reared in pastoral obscurity with his exiled brother, the agricultural deity Balarama (another incarnation of Rama). The pair are sometimes depicted alongside a final escaped sibling, their sister, Subhadra.

As a child, Krishna craved buttermilk, symbolic of sacred nourishment. The cow, of course, is deeply respected in India as provider of unquestioning beneficence, and butter is a distillation of this principle. Krishna spends much of his youth in pursuit of this treat, dreaming up all sorts of ingenious ways to procure it. He is characterized by the principle of *Lila*, or "Divine Play." This precocious behavior helps explain Krishna's great popularity. Who can resist a god who likes to laugh with his devotees? He becomes a living presence to children who listen to stories of him, and his mischievous pranks and playful banter lend themselves perfectly to comic-strip scenarios. There are many children's magazines available in India that colorfully depict Krishna's various adventures.

Like Apollo after a few sips of ambrosia, Krishna springs instantly into Amrita-enhanced adolescence, full of ardor. Both godforms spend much time in pursuit of the lovely specimens of femininity that inevitably grace the mythic landscape, but Krishna is an infinitely more successful suitor than his Greek counterpart. One of his titles is "Stealer of Hearts" in respect of this capacity. Women are enchanted by his celestial beauty and hypnotized into leaving their own households by the transcendental music of his flute.

On the November full moon, known as *Sharad Purnima*, Krishna is supposed to have lured the very gods from the heavens with the melodies of his flute. According to the text of the *Brahmavaivarta*, no fewer than 900,000 devoted women also arrived on the scene, among them Radha. Krishna was happy to frolic with all of his pretty suppli-cants, but it is to Radha that his heart most belongs (see *Invoke the God-dess*). Despite giving his attentions to each and every woman during a thirty-three day dance (Krishna replicates himself, so that each of his partners believes he is wholly hers) he clings to his beloved Radha throughout. She is his *Shakti* and bliss-component, and together they form an entity of unsurpassed spiritual splendour—a channel of divine compassion into the earthly realms.

The meaning of the union of Krishna and the *Gopis*, as his lovers are known, goes beyond an astonishing series of pastoral liaisons. Part of the implication may be that of fertility, as all rural gods clearly are inclined to lovemaking, for obvious reasons, but the main import is much more sophisticated. Krishna represents God-love, and in following him despite taboos, in loving him more than their own husbands and status, his para-mours are proving their unsurpassed devotion to God. They also experi-ence the ecstasy of union with God through the physical and spiritual love known as *Shringara*, which is the root of Tantric practice.

Krishna, likewise, is forced to exude beneficence in every direction, even when he would prefer to confine it to the recipient of his choice. Likewise are the attentions of God drawn hither and thither by the pleas of his supplicants, some perhaps worthier than others. Here we find the root of Krishna's import; he is abundance. The butter and the love he steals represent his breaking with convention, his utter disregard for social structure, because it is only after abandoning the mundane (as do the

Krishna Consciousness devotees) that the eternal might be embraced. A similar lesson is apparent in Kali, but hers is the path of fear transcended, while Krishna's is that of love transcendent. Essentially, Lord Krishna epitomizes the highest ideal of divine love.

Despite the fragile beauty of this blue deity as represented in his icons, Krishna is as strong as he is pretty, as resolute as he is delicate. As with most godforms, he heroically kills a number of demons and pernicious persons in order to preserve Dharma, or righteousness. These demons, such as Madhu, represent blocks of dense energy or negativity, much as crocodiles do in the Egyptian Book of the Dead. Krishna "kills" these monsters with his refined thought-processes, using the powerful yogic techniques discussed in the Bhagavad-Gita. Unlike the many monsters of Greek mythology, which seem to represent little more than obstacles to the heroic quest, those of Hindu and Egyptian origin symbolize a variety of hindrances to the soul's ascension.

The many-headed water serpent Kaliya, for example, was so toxic that cows died after supping from her lake. Krishna dived fearlessly into the waters and emerged dancing and playing his flute on the head of a completely tamed Kaliya. This represents in part Krishna's understanding of the Vedas, which are often depicted as a many-headed python; knowledge which could have been dangerous has been assimilated and made harmonious with him. With Kali—as the root of the serpent's name, we may deduce that the serpent also alludes to the passage of time. Krishna, immortalized by his enlightened nature, is of course immune to the poisons of transience. Sexually speaking, the scenario represents Krishna's move into adulthood; an initiatory feat bound in symbolism with the Kundalini serpent. On a purely mundane level, it demonstrates Krishna's fearless faith in God, the prerequisite to true spiritual progress.

The Bhagavad-Gita describes Krishna's accompaniment of Arjuna onto the battlefield of Kuruksetra. Here he convinces Arjuna, who is understandably reluctant to slay his own brothers and uncles, that it is more important to follow the will of God than be slave to his own emotional attachments. Again, we experience the theme of foregoing the transitory or trivial in favor of the heavenly Will. The philosophy behind this scenario is multifaceted, but two of its most salient features are that Arjuna is of the warrior caste, therefore it is his God-given destiny to fight; secondly, that life and death are an illusion. Thus, if Arjuna wholly believes in his gods, he will kill (and die) in the knowledge that it is the body alone that is slain, not the eternal spirit.

Thus we witness Krishna as a god of philosophy, another of his important roles. He is not simply a deity of love, but is intimately connected with some of the most profound spiritual tracts, still in the process of being fathomed, and which Swami Prabhupada for one would contend cannot be fully understood by those in the mortal condition. (Arjuna himself had difficulty understanding Krishna's import, even though they were best friends and incarnation-long companions!)

Gentle Krishna is equally capable of challenging other gods. The older Vedic deities, such as Indra and Varuna, are superseded in might by the amorous blue god, just as Zeus supersedes Cronos, and Isis disempowers Ra, allowing Horus/Osiris to step into his role. The Old Régime is replaced by the new.

Indra was feared, as was "crooked Cronos," and Krishna suggests to the people that they might worship "Mount Govardhana, whom we love," in lieu of the fearsome warrior deity. The people of Vrindavan, impressed by Krishna's taming and banishment of Kaliya, decide to give this new religious technique a whirl. So they worship a beloved deity and neglect the feared god, bringing seven days and seven nights of Indra's wrath in the form of thunder, lightning, and torrential rain. Krishna, ever ingenious, picks up the mountain with his little finger and uses it to shelter the people, casually maintaining this stance, hand on hip, until Indra's fury ceases. His attitude is cavalier, the stuff romantic heroes are made of. Blithely, Krishna attempts to elicit love, not fear, of God.

By the second century B.C.E., Krishna was on his way to becoming the most popular Hindu godform, and today millions of devotees are quite literally in love with him. Some consciously attempt to emulate his female counterpart, Radha, in order to concentrate their every thought on Krishna and to attract a fragment of his devotion in return. The height of positive emotion he inspires parallels him with the prophet of Christianity, and indeed he is often referred to as the "Christ of the East." Few deities in religious myth have elicited such personal love from their followers.

Because of the overriding popularity of Lord Krishna, he is often considered Purnavatara, the supreme avatar, or the epitome of all other deities. Many Hindus consider Krishna to be God in toto. It is possible for a soul to be assimilated into the living entity that is Krishna on a "partially shared existence" basis. Hindu and Buddhist beliefs differ from some Western perceptions of reincarnation, in that an incarnation or a soul are not closed circuits, but may participate in many sparks of consciousness. Thus it is possible for a hundred former sages, saints, and yogis to combine into a single incarnation in conjunction with an element of the divine. It is likewise possible to share an incarnation on a more mundane level. This might go a little way to explaining multiple personas, although of course all developed spirits are multifaceted to a reasonable degree. Incarnations of a high spiritual quality would certainly not manifest as divergent personalities, but rather be fluent in many cultures and situations, while maintaining a healthy and united overview.

Along with the flute, the two symbols most relevant to Krishna are the fawn and the peacock. The fawn represents both his rural upbringing and gentle, childlike nature, while the peacock symbolizes his royal birth and his omniscient ability. The peacock has a vast lore of its own, all of it pertinent to Krishna. For example, its feet and its squawk are notoriously ugly, representing the material plane. Its plumage, however, is unrivalled in the bird kingdom, and represents a higher level of consciousness.

However, the peacock has long represented pride, and there are few greater obstacles to spiritual development than an excess of vanity. Just as the goddess Sarasvati rides on the back of the peacock, controlling it, so too does Krishna keep the negative aspects of the displaying bird under control; when with him, its beauty is dedicated to God, a declaration of the divine working through nature, and belongs to no individual entity, but to all. In the same manner does Krishna, with his symbolic ability to self-replicate, belong to all his devotees. Finally, the eyes in the peacock feathers represent the mesmerising allure of the material planes. Here we are hypnotized into believing that social status, riches, and transitory pleasures are more important than a search for God. Again, Krishna checks this, rehypnotizing the peacock into remembrance of God, a much sweeter melody than the peacock's squawk of self-interest.

By far the most effective tool for accessing Krishna is the *Maha Mantra.* Concentrating on one of the widely available postcards or paintings of Krishna, while chanting this mantra, cannot fail to forge a living link with the deity. These images may seem rather kitsch at first, with their child-like simplicity and exuberant Technicolor, but this makes them all the easier to visualize. Indeed, Hinduism has been employing creative visualization as a religious technique for thousands of years. Many of the ideas that inspired this book and *Invoke the Goddess* are drawn directly from Hindu devotion and interaction with deities, a daily practice for the devout. How much easier it is to feel personally devoted to a god or goddess when you can actually envisage them! Then your mind has a foundation from which to develop its aspirations and spiritual insights. "Invisible gods" must rely on the forms of their prophets (if, indeed, the religion accepts any), or on a hypothetical sense of their presence, fuzzy at best. In the case of Christianity, a symbol and concomitant visualization of the most astonishing negativity has been construed. An image of Krishna being tortured would be sacrilege; when we are attuned to him, we experience joy.

Krishna is a cult leader, in that he inspires in his devotees an obsessive attachment. Like the lead singer of a teen boy band, he receives adulation, often artless, from his stricken adorers, promising himself to all. He is physically exquisite, faultlessly suave, and full of witty repartee. Just as women fall in love with him, men do too. He is both physical and spiritual with his devotees, and with children he becomes one of them, a pesky playmate, full of schemes and mischief. As an adult, the most effective way to access him is to fall in love with him. Krishna can be all things to all people. Many icons depict him as a child, and the beautiful baby is a form of wide appeal, particularly in India. He may be adored as babe, child, lover, friend, or sage. He is all of these and anything between. No positive emotion is rebuked by Krishna; there is no "wrong" or "right" way to love him, which again explains his popularity.

Because Krishna is a god of *Bhakti*, or devotion, the other most effective means of linking with him is to offer him a devotional gift. The fundamental technique of the Krishna Consciousness movement is to make all principles, actions, and materials Krishna's, thus living in the perpetual awareness of and love for Krishna which is, according to A. C. Bhaktivedanta Swami Prabhupada, the perfection of yogic practice. This is because it denotes an all-encompassing awareness of the Divine Principle, and selfless disinterest in all endeavors. Thus when working, playing, and eating, all is dedicated to Krishna. Also, breathing, creating, and dreaming are dedicated to Krishna. No aspect of being is omitted from this lifelong adoration of the *Purnavatara*.

One of the sayings of Krishna most popular with the Krishna Consciousness movement is:

> *If one of you offers Me with love and devotion a flower, fruit, or water, I will accept it.*

This interpretation of Bhagavad-Gita 9.26 is of supreme importance. It indicates Krishna's accessibility through love, merely; the irrelevance of caste, material means, and religious ceremony in order to link with him mean that he is available to all, at all times.

So a combination of the Maha Mantra thoughtfully chanted and a gift presented with genuine love, as simple or as lovingly crafted as you wish, cannot fail to attract the attentions of beautiful blue-skinned Krishna.

CONTACTING KRISHNA

Krishna may be accessed at any time of the year, day or night.

Incense is always a good start with Hindu deities. Something sweet, such as jasmine, is ideal for Krishna.

Light a candle of yellow or Krishna-blue, and place it at a distance from you so that it will not be extinguished when you powerfully exhale.

Contemplate an image of the beautiful blue god, chant his mantra either out loud or in your head, and offer him a gift. Flowers, a bowl of milk, or simply the smoke from your incense are all suitable. The most important gift is that of an open heart.

VISUALIZATION FOR
SPIRITUAL BEAUTY AND LOVE

The most important thing in this exercise is to quietly sense the all-pervasive power and good will of the Divine. The experience is not action-packed, like some of the other visualizations in this book, but rather, induces a gentle awareness of love made manifest in the world.

Sit cross-legged close to your candle.

Shut your eyes and imagine yourself bathed in brilliant blue light, on the brink of indigo. Visualize it as so bright that you could almost touch it. Its particles seem thick, and move very fast. Breathe this light in and out, concentrating on your third eye area, throat, and then heart. You should experience a feeling of peaceful anticipation, or even excitement. After all, you are about to meet a living love-god.

In front of you, the light begins to coagulate. Flashes of gold pass through it and each time they do, the formulation increases in solidity.

Gradually, the god appears in the aspect that appeals to you most.

See Krishna, in whichever form you prefer, with your inner vision. Whether he appears to you as infant, handsome youth, grown man, warrior, or in a more abstract way such as intelligent light, feel the joy and love he emanates—you will immediately recognize true contact with him by the feeling of happiness and love infusing you.

As your perception of Krishna becomes more intense, listen for his flute. This celestial music draws the soul closer to God and enchants even the most hardened cynics.

If you have envisaged intelligent light, be aware of the myriad forms inside it, the potential of it manifesting as a flesh-and-blood avatar. Compassion dictates that Krishna takes a body from time to time, or that he flashes into the consciousness of mankind dressed in one, to assure us of the fund of Divine Love, which can never run dry. This is needed from time to time to irrigate our parched faith.

Note the elegant fluidity of Krishna's body, almost feminine in form, the kohl-rimmed eyes and infinitely compassionate gaze. His eyes are soft as a fawn's, at once guileless and searing. What a combination of opposites! Yet, they harmonize beautifully. Beauty is certainly the trait that characterizes Krishna.

Between his eyebrows is a U-shaped marking in red. It vibrates with light the color of blood, a resource that Krishna is not afraid to shed. He knows the illusion that is death, and would slay the world to prove that there is no need to fear, were the illusion not necessary for our development. His lips, equally red, are curved into a sweet smile.

Approach the heavenly musician and feel the love and beauty that surrounds him infiltrating your life on every level.

As you concentrate on this celestial unction, offer Krishna your gift—whether it be a flower, a bowl of rice, or better still, your heartfelt devotion. Do not forget that the whole point of this exercise is to increase your spiritual love factor and awareness of the positive forces of the cosmos, so concentrate on the sheer beauty of Krishna until you really sense it. If you tune in properly, you should feel virtually delirious before too long, as if in love.

Cascades of cleansing light seem to be falling around you, astral waterfalls in which your bodies are washed clean of the grime and debris of past hurts, fears, and feelings of hopeless mortality. As the light flows through you, you become increasingly aware of the reality of the gods, manifestations of the same essentially benevolent source. This brings a sense of profound relief, as we all know how difficult it is to maintain a spiritual belief in the midst of humdrum daily living.

However, with this perception comes the realization that nothing, in fact, is humdrum—everything, however apparently mundane, is a manifestation of God and may be understood on a symbolic or magickal level.

Bathe in this stimulating light for as long as you desire, using it to "wash" any particular issues you may have in mind. Reveal everything, however seemingly trivial or unworthy. Krishna can see all anyway, so there is no point in trying to hide your soul's vicissitudes. You may as well expose it to these powerful spiritual waters and watch as it is swept away, leaving the original situation, hopefully, crystal-clear in the afterglow.

The wonderful thing is that you are able to do this in such a sympathetic, uncritical environment. The understanding and compassion that emanate from Krishna are a continual emollient, and they make past mistakes and pains seem necessary but trivial. All fades to insignificance when confronted by this "Big Love."

There is no need to visualize Krishna fading when you have finished; he will either do so himself or, hopefully, stay around you.

To mark the end of the visualization, however, simply open your eyes (if, indeed, they have been shut), and blow out the candle.

The reactions elicited will be different in each case, of course, but one thing is certain: the more frequently and devotedly you contemplate this god, the more often you chant his holy mantra, the stronger will be your link with one of the celestial repositories of spiritual beauty and love.

MUNDANE ARCHETYPES

The Krishna-boy is pretty, effete, and sensitive. Rougher-hewn men tend to think he is gay. He is shy and most likely bisexual, but this can be rather academic as his music and spiritual pursuits take up most of his thoughts. He will be attracted to strong women with confident personalities, often more conventional than he is. This provides him with a grounding much needed in the cruel world.

The Krishna-type loves poetry and philosophy. He has *Rubaiyat of Omar Khayyam* and Kahlil Gibran's *The Prophet* on his bookshelf, and a copy of Derrida, which disappointed him with its superficiality. For him, philosophy must be heartfelt, not mere mental posturing.

Under the bed of the Krishna archetype is a diary, full of obsessive loves, raptures, and swirly doodles, a raft of poetry and songs he's written, and a shoebox full of love letters. Even if these were received when he was eight, he will still cherish them at seventeen.

He believes in reincarnation and the beauty of God made manifest in nature and all living things. He is most likely to be vegetarian. He sings beautifully because he puts his soul into it. He is particularly influenced by Nick Drake and similar acoustic musician-poets, and enjoys Sixties and Indie music in his more frivolous moments.

He is what women call "a beautiful man"; they love him and want to be his friend, but may find him too spineless for a serious relationship. Alternately, he and a girl fall desperately in love, for he is sure to reciprocate any positive emotions sent in his direction. He is always gentle, possibly hirsute in middle age, more confident once he has explored the Buddhist and Hindu paths to which he is almost inevitably drawn.

He travels widely and has rugs and tribal instruments on his walls. He may not marry. If he does, he might well find himself being nagged and grounded by the woman with whom he once tasted ecstasy. This could break his heart.

TAROT CARD
The Lovers

GANESH

Saffron-skirted Ganesh, garlanded with jasmine and hibiscus, emanates an aura as rich and gold as ghee. His jewel-encrusted crown marks him as royal son of Siva and Parvati, the ascetic father and scarlet-saried mother whose domain he has vowed to protect. Axe in hand, he guards the Gateway to their celestial kingdom.

Kohl lines the eyes in the elephant's face, their gaze steady, ever-watchful, not lacking in compassion. He has his mother's gentleness of nature, and his father's ability to destroy. Woe betide the demon or interloper on this sacred space; Ganesh will dispatch him without a second thought to the nether regions where lost spirits wander, transforming the negative energy of the enemy into good by the power of his stomach.

A lotus flower, a bowl of tasty rice balls, and a hand raised in blessing wait to reward the deserving with spiritual insights, physical and spiritual pleasure and nourishment and any number of boons, for Ganesh's bounty is boundless in its limits.

The scholar appeals to him for additional intelligence, and it is granted. The doctor or pharmacist wishes for a new and better practice, and it is given. The enterprising shopkeeper wishes a rival business to be removed, and Ganesh finds a solution that keeps both parties happy. Such are the gifts of the pragmatic elephant-headed god, expert in logistics, most practical of deities.

Ganesh (or Ganesha) is patron of medicine and literature, remover of obstacles, and bringer of luck and success. The striking image of this elephant-headed, four-armed deity is to be found in Hindu surgeries, shops, banks, and head offices, as well as in many portals. Good sense and material ability characterize him; as he is hefty, so does he represent social and financial clout. He protects vested interests and blesses an enterprise.

Ganesh was originally created by Parvati, *Shakti* of Siva, when her husband was absent performing one of his many penances. Parvati was frequently lonely, thanks to Siva's ascetic habits, so she took a portion of her own essence while bathing, and, combining it with a little dust, created Ganesh to guard the door to her private quarters, commanding him to allow absolutely nobody to disturb her bathing rites. However, while beautiful Parvati was at her toilette, Siva returned home unexpectedly, only to find the way to his wife's fond embrace barred by her new son. In a fury, Siva decapitated the overzealous guard. Parvati, horrified, threatened to become Durga/Kali and destroy the Universe unless Siva put his action to rights. So, once his wrath was spent, Siva agreed to resurrect Ganesh by replacing his head with that of the next creature to come their way. This happened to be an elephant, hence Ganesh's chimerical body.

Siva then accepted Ganesh as his own, and Siva, Parvati, and their sons Ganesh and Skanda, the warrior god, represent a popular family unit in Hindu mythology. As well as his many other attributes, Ganesh continued his role as guard, and is subsequently associated with doorways and portals, symbolic of endings and beginnings. He is invoked at weddings, and is an essential presence at the initiation of new enterprises.

It is significant that Siva's one contribution to the creation of Ganesh is his decapitation followed by the replacement of Ganesh's head, the portion of the body in which spiritual consciousness is contained. The act is entirely in keeping with the cycle of creation/destruction with which Siva is particularly associated. Parvati produces a son of singular consciousness, with no ability to reflect; Siva removes the head, destroying the *Maya* illusion, and replaces it with the unforgettable certainty of Siva's eminence, or spiritual truth. Instead of blindly following duty, Ganesh will now have the ability to reflect. He is also accepted into Siva's family, as his son, and thus *becomes* Siva. Similarly are we reminded throughout Hindu lore of our own divinity and unique relationship with God, although this is only after we have been "decapitated" of worldly concerns.

Being a god of yogic austerity, Siva also indicates by removing and replacing of his son's head that individuality is an illusion. Despite having his brain swapped for another, Ganesh remains the same in all but the visual realm, as his spirit, corrected and resurrected by Siva inside the elephantine cranium, is eternal and unaffected by physical circumstance. Because of the head connection, Ganesh is worshipped with reference to intelligence, or *buddhi*, and his mantra is frequently written across exam papers in respect of this quality.

Worshipped as the purveyor of worldly wisdom, Ganesh is famed for his ability to think around a problem, providing a succinct and brilliant alternative to the conventional answer. He and his brother Skanda once decided to race one another around the world. Skanda dashed off on his peacock, flying as fast as he could, while Ganesh and his rat simply ambled round their parents, Siva and Parvati, thus encircling the Universe in one easy gesture.

Where other deities ride the eagle Garuda, or a swan, a peacock, or a noble feline when they wish to travel, Ganesh has for his steed the lowly mouse or rat. This symbolizes his ability to protect interests by controlling pestilence; to the shopkeeping class with whom he is particularly popular, the rat is a familiar nuisance. Elephants are renowned for their fear of rodents, but Ganesh is immune to such concerns. The unlikely steed also represents his divine levity. After all, no potbellied elephant that was not divine could ride upon a rat. Despite his considerable strength and size, he levitates at will.

Ganesh's portly proportions, reminiscent of the Chinese god of luck (the laughing Buddha), reflect his wisdom and ability to assimilate the material world and absorb problems, represented by dense matter. Thus, rather than indicating gluttony, his fat stomach signifies transformative and intermediary skills. Many Indian gurus are similarly potbellied; indeed, not just Indian, but American aspirants such as Adi Da evince the same feature. Some claim that this is due to a particular type of psychic energy (or *Siddhi* power), which causes its host to augment in size, much as Dion Fortune did as her mediumistic skills increased. On a more banal level, the idea from an Indian perspective is that the nation wishes to sustain its spiritual masters, thus a well-fed guru in an undernourished country reflects the supreme importance to its people of the spiritual principle.

Ganesh *Lambodar,* "of the potbelly," attained his size in an entertaining manner. King Kubera, Lord of Worldly Wealth, was irritated by the asceticism and self-denial of the gods, and decided to invite Siva and Parvati to supper in order to tempt them with the abundance of his cuisine and the finery of his material possessions. Refusing, Siva and Parvati instead sent Ganesh, at whom the king laughed rudely, announcing that he could provide food for a hundred-thousand puny boys like him. Ganesh thus began to eat, and to eat and to eat, his appetite apparently knowing no bounds. Before very long, little Ganesh had eaten the cowed king out of house and home. The latter was forced to beg Siva to make Ganesh stop. Thus, with the aid of potbellied Ganesh, did Kubera learn not to boast. This parable reflects Ganesh's Siva-given role as destroyer of the ego-principle.

In a similar manner, Ganesh's other oversized features represent his various capacities. His ears, of course, indicate his ability to listen, and to hear the requests of his supplicants, his mouth and stomach his ability to break down and absorb all that life can throw at him, and his trunk signifies his obstacle-removing aspect. It is also a sensitive extra limb, which, along with his four arms, represents his versatility and capability in any situation.

The implements held by Ganesh are symbolic of the cauterization of wrongful attachment (the chopper), binding mankind to the sacred truth (the rope), rewarding him for effort and courage (the bowl of rice), and blessing (the raised and empty hand).

Ganesh is one of the minor deities who represents the limited manifestations of the Supreme God. He is connected with lunar cycles, the bright of which are propitious, and the dark ill-omened (as in most cultures).

The connection with the moon emanates from a strange tale, though possibly not in quite the form it originally carried. One night, when Ganesh was suffering from indigestion after testing his potbelly to the full, his mount bolted at the sight of a snake, catapulting Ganesh into the air and then onto the ground, where his stomach suffered further damage. The moon, watching, burst out laughing at the god's comic escapade, whereat Ganesh, in a fury, ripped off one of his tusks and threw it at the silver orb with a potent curse, thus depriving it of the perpetual fullness of its light. So, when bright and full, the moon is curse-free, but when waning and dark, it suffers the wrath of the god of luck.

Ganesh is the ideal deity to whom to appeal for the removal of an obstacle that stands between you and your aspirations—this is particularly relevant to scholarly and career-related issues. He may also be approached to aid the "digestion" of a problem, helping you to assimilate and come to terms with it.

CONTACTING GANESH

As with all Hindu deities, a good way of formulating a link is to take advantage of one of the many vivid images of the gods. A postcard or a statue is ideal. If you can garland the latter, all the better.

A sweet incense will also help; jasmine, hibiscus, or ylang-ylang, for example.

It is also helpful to chant, either out loud or mentally, the mantra of the deity in order to access their essence. The *Gayatri* or Vedic Mantra of Ganesh is:

> *OM Ekadantaya Vidmahe Vakratundaya Dheemahi,*
> *Tanno Danti Prachodayat.*

—Quite a mouthful for those of us of Western origin. An easier alternative is the Bija Mantra:

> *OM Shri Ganeshya Namah.*

The best time to approach Ganesh is when the moon is waxing or full, the best psychological condition is to be "on the brink" of something, and the ideal location is in a portal (such as a hall), or at least, in front of a door.

VISUALIZATION FOR REMOVING NEGATIVITY

Once you have performed the preparations described above, bow to the image of Ganesh (either mentally or literally), and sit cross-legged before it.

Imagine the situation you wish to remove as a cloud of dark smoke or substance issuing from your solar plexus. If there is no specific obstacle in your way, simply imagine any negative feelings that might be holding you back from success exiting your body as described.

As you exude this substance, visualize a cloud of golden light beginning to form between you and the doorway. As it gathers momentum, it becomes larger and larger until it nearly reaches the ceiling. Then, gradually solidifying, it reveals the outline and then shape of a four-armed, potbellied man up to the neck, and the head and trunk of an elephant.

The more negativity you give out, the stronger and brighter the image of Ganesh becomes. It seems to be gaining strength from your emotional fallout.

Before long, there stands before you a radiant Ganesh, solid as a rock, from his jewel-encrusted crown of gold to his saffron silk-clad legs and feet, around which lustrous anklets jingle. His arms are moving, and as he turns his palms to face your miasma, the tools and dish of rice he held formerly fade to nothing.

As he moves his limbs, you notice that Ganesh's nails are painted. Now, however, you cannot see them, as he is holding up his palms toward you. Each palm is painted at the center with red henna in the shape of a circle surrounded by petals.

As soon as Ganesh directs his open palms to you, the foul stuff surrounding you begins to flow up and into the center of the red henna flower painted at their center. It drains away from you, and into him. The steady ebb speeds up, and Ganesh licks his lips. To your surprise you realize he is actually enjoying the process.

Now watch Ganesh suck your problems up and instantly "digest" them in his fat belly. As much as you give out, he can easily assimilate and translate into a positive. If your negative substance has become a solid, he may use his trunk to encompass it before eating it whole. It is child's play to Ganesh; your problems seem very insignificant indeed when they can be so simply imbibed by the god.

Continue with this process until all of your doubts and fears have been removed.

When you have finished, or rather, when Ganesh has, he looks at you with his slanting, heavily lashed eyes, and, it seems, from between the brows on which an elaborate bindi of red is painted. His massive ears hang about his shoulders and remind you that he is always there to listen to your problems and proposed ventures. He takes pride in removing obstacles; it is a two-way deal.

He begins to fade, off to find another feed.

His superfat belly is the last thing to vanish, reminding you that there is plenty of room in there for future use.

Thank Ganesh, and return to your room when you are ready.

An offering of a sweet or some rice would not go amiss at this point; just leave it in front of the image and mentally offer it to Ganesh. It's probably tastier to him than your problems, and might just finish them off nicely.

VISUALIZATION FOR CAREER AND BUSINESS SUCCESS (ESPECIALLY AGAINST THE ODDS)

As above, sit in front of a door or, better still, in a hallway.

Breathe in several lungfuls of golden light. Center yourself at your solar plexus, by concentrating the light and your thoughts at the point beneath your ribcage and above your stomach.

Now, visualize the obstacles you have to surmount as an elephant. The great bulking mass seems impossible to navigate or control. It sits before you, intractable as a bank overdraft.

Your aspirations, however, are but a tiny mouse in comparison. They seem quite feeble in the face of the circumstances you need to surmount.

Breathe in more of the light until you feel almost solid gold yourself. As you do so, notice that the elephant begins to change color. The gray of its ancient-looking hide is gradually beginning to glisten into gold.

Keep breathing in this way until the dull mass of your former obstacles has transformed into one of radiance.

Now, concentrate on your solar plexus, and send out to the elephant all of your hopes for your future. Think of the hard work, money, and time that you've invested in your project, and of how much you want it to succeed. Send all of your Will for this venture to pay off in bright golden rays from your solar plexus into the gray, bulky mammal.

As it receives the energy of your aspirations, the elephant rises on to its hind legs, and you notice that the gold of its legs is actually the brilliant saffron of a gold-embroidered *dhoti*, and that the rest of it has faded to pale lotus-pink. Another set of arms appears and conjoins the first at the shoulder. Each perfumed hand holds an implement; axe, plate of rice balls, lotus, and the last is raised in blessing.

A garland of sweet-smelling jasmine hangs around Ganesh's neck. He is richly adorned with exquisite jewelry. His crown is almost outshone by the luster of a pair of slanting brown eyes looking at you from between a couple of enormous flapping ears. An elaborate wine-red bindi sits on his ponderous forehead.

So, this is what your ventures have become. Can't be bad!

As you think this, the image begins to fade.

Before you there appears a garlanded archway. It is on the other side of this, you perceive, that your hopes will solidify. Here, they are just wishful thinking. Beyond the archway, they become Absolutes.

The problem is, how to get your rapidly fading Ganesh to move through the portal.

Ah, the rodent. Almost forgotten, but still here, quite definitely. The trick is to get Ganesh to ride the little beastie through the festooned doorway.

You will have to use all the strength of your willpower to levitate Ganesh onto the rat or mouse. It may seem difficult, but if Ganesh can ride a rat as a steed, anything is possible, your intended project not least.

Concentrate on the feat until your aspiration-god is seated on the tiny rodent. To your surprise, the mouse seems hardly to notice. It looks at the door, sniffs the air for a second, and then scampers through the portal, bearing your hopes aboard its furry back.

As it passes through, be aware of your aspirations becoming realities in the future. Now that they are blessed by the god of good luck and success in enterprise, they cannot fail.

Did you find it easy to lift Ganesh onto his tiny steed? If it was very difficult—or impossible—the obstacles may be greater than the payoff.

Was your mouse nimble and lively beneath Ganesh? Or, worst case scenario, if it was crushed by him, the enterprise is impractical or unlikely to succeed. Perhaps a more pragmatic approach would help. Logical thinking combined with flashes of inspiration are the food of this deity's mind. Feed it with great, practical thoughts, and Ganesh will respond. He is particularly interested in long-term ventures, family businesses, and the like. So, if you were unsuccessful with him, reconsidering the project in this light may well bring a viable alternative.

MUNDANE ARCHETYPES

The Ganesh-type is always stocky, and sometimes obese. He turns to food when upset or depressed, finding comfort and energy in it. In his stronger aspects, however, he is often jovial and confident, a rosy-cheeked boy or expansive, hospitable man.

Ganesh does not think deeply, and the more sensitive envy his ability to laugh at the complexities of life. He believes in happiness through simplicity and material objects—money, house, good food—and that these lead to the other sustainers of life—status and companionship. He is often a successful and popular businessman, one who has proved his mettle over the years and who is not shy in taking his clients to expensive restaurants or showing his appreciation of others through gifts. He can be coarse in this respect, with a love of showy gold jewelry, expensive watches, etc., and the more spiritually and intellectually refined will consider him crude. In England he might be termed "nouveau riche."

However, no one can doubt the nous of this potbellied man. He can see his way round the most immovable obstacles, making him a welcome addition to any project, particularly involving construction or expansion. He loves his family and, so long as he is gainfully employed, can be a fun and inspiring father. However, if lacking in a project or channel for his abundant energies, he may become a resentful couch potato and lose himself in one-dimensional perceptions. Then we witness the slobbish side of this otherwise smart-thinking individual.

TAROT CARDS

Nine of Cups, Ace of Pentacles, Four of Pentacles

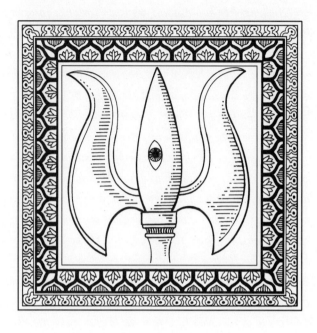

SIVA

The Ganges pours from Siva's hair in seven sacred streams, carrying sacraments in its holy potent flow. Ash, which has dusted his head for years, floats as flotsam on the dark and luminous waters.

His skin is the Himalayan snow, ice-cold with renunciation, each peak a feat of Will over matter, a monument to self-mortification carved out by centuries of stalwart effort. The blue sky is his face, as dark as a storm cloud at the throat where the poison of the Cosmos is trapped, corked forever against the demons who would use it to destroy Dharma and mankind.

Behind his head rears the thousand-headed cobra, its hood protecting him from sun and snow. The crescent moon glimmers in his hair like a fish trapped in a net, and in the background hangs another moon, huge and astral, shining full on the haunted yogic mountains. Gurus abide here, youthful ancients like holy Babaji, wizened sadhus contorted in devotion, levitating mystics who can walk in two worlds at once, occult masters and chanting mantrics who keep the cosmic motor running, saintly beings who live and die in bleak obscurity, but bless the world of men with their very breath.

In Siva's domain the sound of OM is audible in the steep inclines that are acts of devotion petrified, and in cold, dark caves, lined with tiger fur, it finds its echo. Sometimes the peacefulness of this retreat enrages him; a hundred thousand years of meditation can make man and god alike crave the wilder side of life. Then, Siva arises, unravelling the legs bent so long in sacred lotus posture, and the mountains shake as the power crackles from his limbs.

Four ash-encrusted arms fan out to touch the sky, remembering their fluency of movement. Ecstatic with the change, the Lord begins to dance, slowly at first, in long movements like the serpents, which are his jewelry, then faster, and with menacing intent.

His face grows darker; where once was pallor, life-force spreads across his physiognomy like a bruise. His third eye clicks open, and a thousand trees are incinerated as it takes its primal glance.

As news of Siva's awakening spreads through the ether, his retinue gathers. From cemetery and morgue comes a storm of lost souls, whirling its way up the mountain with a high pitched freakish groan, a sound to freeze the blood of those who live. Evil spirits are attracted to the fray, and with these come the possessed and the spiritually dispossessed, the insane, and shrieking women tearing at their hair. All the thieves and criminals of India hear the call of their Lord, and add themselves to his ghastly crew. Together they whirl wildly down the mountain, thunderous blue-skinned Siva and a million ghosts and phantasms and chanting sorcerers and women beating at their breasts like those in grief.

He will wipe the world away and bring its struggling souls to rest in his body, monumental dancing Siva, trident swirling, arms like blades now as he gathers speed and runs screaming, drooling down the mountain. Every creature that hears this sound dies instantly, shedding the shell of flesh which is the gods' favorite trick, and finding sweet refreshment in the fountain of life that is the inner essence of frightful-seeming Siva.

His thoughts are irrevocable, for though he still sits in Samadhi on that icy mount, and though he has merely dreamed the day of our destruction, his mind sets the wheels of Maya into action, and, once triggered, no one can turn them back.

Now Siva will slice up the world, and then with lingam and yoni conjoined, conceive another, purer, cleaner than the last.

Demons will not know this new place, nor will the possessed or spiritually dispossessed. The new Yuga will be blessed by Siva and by the Kalki Avatara, final incarnation of Vishnu, an era of virtue and of realization of God. For the act of creation is as natural to him as that of destruction, and the gods play with poles of duality like children playing with torches and shadows.

Once this is done, he will return to his palace, to luxuriant-haired Parvati in her scarlet sari glistening with gold, to his dear sons Ganesh and Skanda, and tell them all about what he's done at work today.

With his handsome body besmeared with ash, matted hair piled high, live serpent jewelry, and loincloth of tiger skin, Siva is one of the most striking manifestations of the Hindu pantheon. This holy ash is actually the remnants of burnt cow-dung, known as *vibhuti*, the cow representative of the holy Mother of Creation, the fire of the male principle. This male-female balance is all-important to the symbolism of Siva, who through the gender dynamic (or Siva-Shakti relationship), describes the interaction of pure consciousness and the active, creative principle. Siva's devotees are often found heavily powdered in this fine, sweet-smelling substance. They have purified themselves in the fires of self-denial and hardship. Unlike Krishna, who emanates bounty, Siva exudes asceticism and denial of the senses. His path is that of strict self-control, and his personal power is that of *Tapas*, or annihilation.

Siva is the destructive principle in the trinity of Vishnu-Brahma-Siva. Vishnu creates life and preserves it, Siva brings cycles to a close, and between them exists Brahma, uniting the opposites and creating a balanced state that facilitates life as we know it. During the brief span of each incarnation, we are forced to suffer in order to learn, causing the twelfth-century Hindu poet and Siva devotee Basavanna to rail:

> *Siva, you have no mercy.*
> *Siva, you have no heart.*
> *Why why did you bring me to birth,*
> *Wretch in this world,*
> *Exile from the other?*

This sensibility evinces the lack of fatalism found in the bulk of Hindu literature, and certainly contrasts with the unquestioning endurance (and fear of *hubris*) evident in the other religions studied here, Greek and Egyptian. It is the cry of a devotee working, like Siva, outside the established order. The rhetoric may, of course, be a poetic ploy, or Basavanna (or his translator) may be echoing the typically Judeo-Christian sentiments of the era in which he was writing ("Why have you forsaken me?"). Either way, the lines reflect the horror felt, even by one devoted to God, at the apparently dire mortal condition. Between these cycles, we may "sleep in Siva," or be united with God; but duality is periodically forced upon us in the shape of a body and life on the stage of Maya. However, the poet instantly answers his own question confirming Siva's loving care throughout this tribulation:

> *As a mother runs*
> *close behind her child*
> *with his hand on a cobra or a fire,*
> *the lord of the meeting rivers*
> *stays with me*
> *every step of the way*
> *and looks after me.*

We are perpetually under the loving scrutiny of Siva's third eye, according to Basavanna and other Sivaites. Sai Baba was said to demonstrate this principle by manifesting quantities of *vibhuti* both personally and, in the most unlikely places, such as on and behind portraits of saints in North London, and anywhere else inhabited by his devotees. Holy ash in the midst of daily life represented the perpetual loving scrutiny of Siva, and, indeed, of Sai Baba himself, who claimed to know his flock's every deed and thought. With one glance from his *Ajna* optic, Siva can blast demons into oblivion; so, caring for mortals, even as a mother guards her child, is not a problem. This is another symbolic property of the ash.

It is interesting to see Siva perceived in this maternal role, when he seems such a fierce god, with his pale skin dusted in the residue of purification, his necklace of skulls like Kali's reflecting his activities as Reaper. He is usually depicted in meditation or slaying the monsters of impure thought. However, just as he has his *Shakti* or feminine counterpart (in this case, Parvati), so does he evince a maternal aspect in relation to his supplicants. Hindu gods are very versatile. Just as Krishna may be approached as child, lover, friend, or guru, so is Siva father, mother, and god. He is lord of the ascetics, and many *sadhus* (holy ascetics) imitate his appearance, usually without the tiger skin. They also aspire to attain boons and spiritual grace through penance and denial, which entail such bizarre activities as burying their heads in sand for days on end, not moving for years, holding the arms out until they are in agony, and so forth. These activities are believed to create a spiritual "heat" from which arises the power to perform psycho-spiritual miracles known as *Siddhi* powers.

Siva's weapon is the trident of iron, which was originally smelted by the heretic Lords of Darukavana when they became jealous of the attraction their wives felt for the god. They conspired together to slay Siva with dark magic, creating a deer to distract him, a ferocious tiger to consume him, and vicious weapons cursed to bring Siva harm. Siva slayed the tiger in a trice and took its pelt as a trophy, touched the deer and kept it about his person as a totem, and took the iron to form his trident. Finally he celebrated his victory with a celestial dance. Thus did he reverse the Karma inflicted on him, making himself thrice-blessed where once he was thrice-cursed.

Siva's natural habitats are the Himalayas, and cremation and burial grounds. His retinue includes ghosts and vampires and, like Kali, he haunts the abodes of the processes of dissolution for which he is responsible. He defies all material wealth, and his followers may be found *digambara*, or "sky clad," in the cemetery chanting his mantra, deep in meditation. The drum, another of Siva's symbols, echoes his mantric aspects, through which the soul is liberated by sacred rhythm.

Siva's merciful aspect is symbolized by his bright blue neck. When the sea of milk was being churned at the beginning of creation, the celestial drink *Amrita* was created. However, alongside it, a terrible poison was produced, strong enough to destroy the whole of mankind. Although a destroyer rather than preserver, Siva compassionately swallowed the poison himself, causing great personal discomfort. Parvati, his loving wife, feared that he might die of it, and so blocked the path from his throat to his stomach. The potent poison thus stayed lodged in Siva's throat, imbuing it with its deadly color. This immunity explains in part his role as supreme physician.

Siva's mount is the white bull Nandi, who is worshipped in India as another god. When Siva takes an animal form, which he does frequently, it is mostly as a bull. The connotations of agriculture and fertility evident in Nandi bring us to Siva's ithyphallic aspect, in which he is worshipped as the lingam, or erect phallus. A peculiar attribute, one might think, for a god of asceticism, especially one who incinerates Kama, the god of love, with a glance of his third eye. Siva refuses to accept his ordained *Shakti*, Parvati, until she has undergone severe austerities and thus proved herself to be a suitable companion on a spiritual level. However, the *lingam* is crucial to the dance of life of which Siva is lord, and to the process of rebirth, and thereby states which are finite—Siva's domain. This symbol of natural creative energy is teamed with the female *yoni* to represent the source of creative power.

Siva dances in two ways; the Dance of Life when his positive energy is bubbling up, and the terrible Dance of Destruction, when he raves likes a madman and becomes the antithesis of what we regard as healthy and desirable. Of course, both of these aspects are needed to preserve existence. Qabalistically speaking, Siva perfectly represents the extremes of Geburah (destruction) and Chesed (life-nurturing mercy), between which lies the state of effective existence.

These poles of severity and mercy, restriction and abundance, are represented in Hinduism by the currents *Ida* and *Pingala*. The yogi aims to control his relations with both currents, often through breathing exercises. As Lord of Yoga, Siva is essential to this process, and thus to the process of spiritual liberation it engenders. In Kundalini Yoga the practitioner seeks the union of the Siva and Shakti within, the energetic union of male and female principles, conceptual and active forces working in harmony. The union of Siva and Parvati symbolizes the reconciliation of opposites, which is a key to Siva's iconography. However, the most important aspects of this process occur on the subtle planes, befitting Siva, as master of asceticism, to the role, despite its powerful sexual nature. The phallus of Siva is not merely the basic fertility emblem of the original pagan, but an "Ace of Rods" on the inner planes, denoting communication between the celestial and the mortal, remembrance of our purpose on this plane, and spiritual progression. Siva's physical attributes exist merely to help the mind fix on the pure and boundless consciousness that is his true being.

Another famous image of Siva depicts him prostrate beneath Kali, who dances her own bloodthirsty jig. Rather than being subjugated by her, as the image at first suggests, Siva is again acting out of compassion for humanity. Having slain the demon Mahishasura, Kali is drunk with bloodlust, and threatens to destroy mankind before her thirst is sated. Siva, in this instance perceived as her beloved husband, places himself in her way in order to bring her to her senses. She stops, but the moment at which she perceives Siva, yet is still astride him, has come to symbolize the union of male and female principles of creative force.

As well as haunting the battleground and mortuary, Siva presides over thieves and robbers. This may seem a strange patronage for a god of Penance, but thieves, like Siva, are working outside the established order in a destructive-creative framework. The Siva we know today developed from Rudra, the Vedic archer whose arrows bring indiscriminate disease and death, whose aspect was dark and terrible, and to whom criminals would have naturally been drawn.

A complete contrast to this aspect of Siva's nature is the frequently depicted role of "family man" which he plays with Parvati (or, further back, Sati, the "perfect wife" from whose legend arises the tradition of the self-immolation of widows), Skanda, and often little Ganesh. He wears the *tripundraka* on his forehead, the three horizonal stripes of sandalwood and ash often imitated by his followers. On the palm of his hand is the holy syllable *OM*, the source of all manifestation.

Another emblem of significance to Siva is the moon, the crescent of which he wears in his hair. Legend says that the moon floated to the top of the sea of milk when the Universe was being churned, and Siva took it for a diadem. The lunar symbol befits Siva's role as creator (new moon), preserver and enlightener (full moon), and seemingly insane destroyer (waning and dark moons). It is a clear reference to contemplation and solitude. Siva is sometimes depicted as white as moonlight or Himalayan snow, colors reflected by many of his devotees who smear their entire bodies with vibhuti and sandalwood paste. A gathering of sadhus, such as occurs once every ten years in Benares, can look much like the film *Night of the Living Dead*, with matted-haired yogis with wild staring eyes, often contorted from years of penance, walking around as white as sheets with ash and dust. There could of course be no more appropriate homage to Siva in his role as resuscitator of souls (bringing self-realization through yoga and devotional practice), and destroyer of Maya.

Once, during a game of dice, Parvati asked Siva who the sun and the moon really were. He replied that they were his two eyes, and Parvati, for a joke, placed her hands over them. The world was plunged into darkness and chaos. As punishment for this tomfoolery, Parvati gained her Kali-aspect, and was temporarily exiled to earth encased in it. This is one of the rare occasions on which Parvati did not "win" the game. Usually, she is an insurmountable opponent, allowing Siva to win only the occasional round (why would he play if he never won?). His usual prize is a kiss, the next might be an embrace, and the next . . . well, the game is a celestial love-play. However, when Parvati wins, she takes Siva's weapons—his trident, discus, even his faithful bull Nandi. There are many illustrations of Siva in this distressing predicament. The famous caves at Ellora in India are rich with imagery of this play between the god and goddess. They are mimicked in Hindu wedding lore, in which husband and wife are encouraged to play games of chance together, and the husband allows the wife to win. Parvati likewise completely denudes Siva of his ritual paraphernalia, and "cuts him down to size." Even the god of destruction is subject to the vicissitudes of Fate.

Because of their gaming trysts, Parvati and Siva frequently argue. When Siva loses, his bad temper causes him to play some pretty dirty tricks, and Parvati, in her turn, becomes petulant. One South Indian tale tells of how Siva and his wife were playing at *cenne* (a game involving collecting what we would probably call "pieces of pie" to fill a board), and

Parvati was beating Siva as usual. He began to complain of giddiness and nausea, so the faithful wife went to fetch him some milk. When she returned, he had reversed the board so that the "lucky side" was facing him. In fury, she kicked it over. Exasperated, he cursed her finest sari, commanding that black ants eat it, and stormed out of their home.

Parvati smeared her face with black ash, removed her finery, and replaced it with rags. Running to the forest, where she knew her furious husband would be roaming, she sat and pretended to be an Untouchable.

Siva soon discovered her, picking lice from her hair, and in his anger and desire to get back at Parvati, failed to realize that this was his wife in disguise, and spent two days making love to her.

On returning home, Siva was interrogated about his actions, and in time-honored manner, denied everything. However, it soon became apparent that Parvati "knew," so he accepted her offering of milk and water, relented, and apologized.

Like many Hindu (and Greek) myths, this legend is based on a timeless domestic scenario. Just as Hera henpecks Zeus and is well aware of what he is up to, even if she cannot stop it, Parvati displays a thorough knowledge of her husband's character, and must operate cleverly within that framework to subtly dominate him. There are moral lessons of forgiveness and mutual tolerance in the tale, and an impasse is reached, which will last until the next power-struggle arises. The couple portray a timeless gender dynamic.

One of the main problems apparent in the "marriage" of Siva and Parvati, is his addiction to solitary meditation and hashish, both of which he deems of greater importance than his domestic life with Parvati. The point of this is that God's Will must always come above mundane concerns, just as Krishna must leave Radha in order to perform his duties as avatar. The hashish represents an abstract state of mind, which others can neither follow or participate in. The individual's relationship with the Divine is unique, as is the path he must tread to reach it. Siva's antisocial, spiritual inclinations are simply something Parvati must come to terms with.

It falls to Parvati, therefore, to keep the relationship going. She is intelligent and spiritual herself, but she realizes that unless she equals or excels Siva's asceticism, he will never hold her in high regard. Therefore she does just that. For the sake of love, she undergoes every penance and hardship, chants to and meditates on God continually, and eventually attains Siva's admiration. He even acknowledges that she has, in some respects, exceeded him.

Siva is therefore a suitable godform to whom to appeal for strength in denying oneself something. This should be a habit, emotional or physical, which will leave us freer once it has been shed. Diets do not count unless they are spiritually relevant (the undergoing of a small fast, for example); vanity is definitely not the right motive for this god (see Artemis in *Invoke the Goddess* for ideas to help change body-shape). Giving up neurotic and emotional addictions, or physical habits, however, are tasks with which Siva can help.

CONTACTING SIVA

The best time of the year to contemplate Siva is winter, but any waning or dark moon will do. Night is best, and in solitude. Sandalwood incense will help get you on a suitable wavelength.

Light a dark blue or purple candle, and place it in a safe place parallel to the bridge of your nose.

Assume the yogic posture most comfortable to you. If you cannot manage lotus posture, sitting cross-legged on the floor will do.

If you wish to "go the whole hog," which is not essential but may aid a more vivid visualization, you could also smear a little ash on your face, a peculiar idea to the Western mind, but one whose symbolism amply befits the god we are approaching. Alternately, draw the *tripundraka* (three horizontal lines and a symbolic third eye) of Siva on your forehead.

If you can, perform this meditation when hungry. Better still, undergo a fast for a few days prior to it. If you work, or are required to exert your body on day-to-day basis, be moderate in this. If you are fortuitously free of such concerns, you can be as extreme as you like. Siva is, after all, god of renunciants and ascetics.

VISUALIZATION FOR SELF-CONTROL OR GIVING UP A VICE

You are in the wilderness. Wild beasts can be perceived watching you from the undergrowth, and nearby, a giant cobra winds itself around a tree. Ghosts, too, haunt these godless wilds, and a feeling of menace keeps you forging your way ahead. Your goal? The pristine Himalayas, which you can see in the distance, like remote paternal arms waiting to embrace and protect you.

However, it seems to be a very long journey before you reach their sanctuary.

The night is closing in. The twilight is blue, electric. The forest seems to comprise your darkest fears. In shadowy bowers lurk people from your past, those who have hurt you—and evil seems to press in from every side. It is as if the wrongs done to you in this life were carefully synchronized to cause you maximum damage. The weaknesses engendered in you seem inevitable, inescapable.

Misery closes in on you. With a sudden shock, you notice that your enemies are laughing at you from the foliage and gossiping about your wretched state like excited, evil monkeys. You are unsure as to whether you can bear it—you have half a mind to end the visualization here and now.

Resolving to be strong in the cause of self-control, you begin to consciously fight any fear you may feel. Not only this, but you determine to break the harmful cycle you have been caught up in. Be sure to invest this part of the visualization with genuine positive intent.

As you do so, the beasts and phantasms instantly fade into symbols. Mentally note what they become; they will be of use to you when interpreting your experience later.

Propel yourself toward the snow-peaked purple Himalayas in the distance. This may take a considerable amount of effort, so exert yourself until you are able to reach one of the mountains.

Feel how the atmosphere thins out and becomes more spiritually refined as you begin to ascend. In one of the most remote caves, Siva is sitting in meditation, his limbs rigid with disuse, his hair a nest of serpents, his blue skin partially obscured by the dust of ages. The mere thought of encountering the Great Ascetic sends shockwaves through your aura. Yet it is essential to your own progress that you supplicate the powerful Lord of Yogis.

Ascend the mountain in whatever way seems natural to you. Levitation is always a handy technique at such times, though if you prefer to visualize yourself walking or travelling by any other means, do so. The main point is to ascend the purple rock, the white snows, the lonely terrain whose altitude is already making you feel faint.

Rise up and up, breathing in the pure air, which appears to your inner eye somehow purple and white, or blue and white—up and up, the atmosphere seeming to cleanse you just through immersion in it. Seek out Siva amongst the barren crags and ancient fallen rocks.

When you are close to the god astrally, you will feel a tingle of excitement at the very least. Propel yourself toward the source of this sensation.

As you draw close to Siva, the air becomes very dark blue and cold, yet simultaneously it nurtures you. The sensation is peculiar, but not distressing. Your inner vision will expand dramatically.

Siva's eyes are closed in divine meditation, but his third eye glares down at you.

Present your situation and problems to the vibrant blue deity. He towers over you in all senses, but you know that he feels compassion for mankind—his color is witness to this—and that includes you. The gods require human suffering in order to be graceful. It is their pleasure to grant boons and terminate anguish. Note the faint smile on the Yogi's parched lips; though he is in Samadhi, still he perceives your plea.

Supplicate and interact with him for as long as you wish. This will be an entirely personal experience.

When you are ready, leave a token of your esteem with the god—an imaginary garland, perhaps, or better still, the promise to give up a vice, such as a habit or emotional addiction—and retreat. Travel back down the mountain, into the forest, and then into your room.

Once you have contemplated your experience for a little while, write it down. Do not forget to mention and interpret the symbols of your "melted fears" from the forest scenario. These can greatly aid you in discovering the root of these issues.

If you found it difficult to push yourself from the forest to the mountains, you need to discipline yourself more. If you were swiftly propelled toward the distant abode of the celestial ascetic, you have gained strength through hardship.

Now it is time to use your own willpower, the hallmark of a Sivaite, to free yourself from the shackles of your past.

MUNDANE ARCHETYPES

The Siva-man is "alternative" and proud of it. He may have one close female friend, possibly his sister, or similar male companions, but most people find him aloof. He is often of impressive stature, may wear his hair in dreadlocks, or any other style that expresses his individuality and which he can carry off with apparent ease, and he dresses (often scruffily) to make a point.

The Siva archetype is usually cool and detached; it is through drugs that he finds himself verging on the sociable. Like his Hindu counterpart, the Siva-man smokes hashish and finds it therapeutic and thought-enhancing. During the day, and when at work, he is likely to drink too much coffee and smoke himself out with hand-rolled cigarettes. He is blithe about his health, claiming that stress is the main killer in this era.

Because of his erratic lifestyle, caused more by nocturnal thinking or socializing than by anything physically demanding, Siva is often thin, and usually wired, but rarely in an easily accessible way. He can be bad tempered and argumentative, often provoking gigantic blow-outs with the woman in his life. He is likely to have children young, probably several, whom he treats with genuine interest one minute (taking them to music festivals and the like), followed by sudden bouts of fatigue the next. Their mothers are almost always hippie-types. The general populace bores him, and he can be snappy with strangers when it would behoove him to be polite.

Siva rarely becomes overattached to a partner, and is equally casual about jobs, abodes, and even his friends. He does not require much of anything to get by.

TAROT CARDS
The Tower, Death, The Hermit

HANUMAN

Hanuman, lord of the monkeys, bravest of warriors and most devout of disciples, commands his armies with wisdom and the strength of Righteousness. No demon can outwit him, for he sees around corners in dark minds and throws them into light relief.

Blazing a trail of glory behind him, Hanuman ransacks the cities of the Unrighteous and, ever gallant, plucks from the flames of falling timbers the innocents there imprisoned. Sita herself was stolen from Ravana's polluting grip by the brave disciple-god and returned to Rama, her husband and the leading light of Hanuman's devotion.

Hanuman, resplendent in golden armor, swift and quick-witted, amasses glory and places it instantly at the lotus feet of his beloved guide and master, Rama. All that Hanuman does he dedicates to Rama, and all of the bounty he amasses is placed in Rama's treasure troves.

To have his gifts and services accepted is the only reward Hanuman seeks. Thus does he ever grow in strength, and in the strength of Righteousness.

Hanuman was born a monkey, but through action dedicated to the gods, particularly Rama and Sita, he attained divinity. He is one of the heroes of the Mahabharata, helping Rama to wrest his wife, Sita, from the demon king Ravana. Like many of the Hindu gods, he has a sense of humor and mischief, which never detracts from the seriousness with which he performs his religious duties. Hanuman represents obedience to guru and God without questioning, and courage borne of absolute faith.

Hanuman, son of Anjana and the wind god Parvana (sometimes known as *Vayu*, "air"), is said to be an incarnation of Siva. Anjana had been cursed to assume the body of a monkey until giving birth to Siva, and in the time-honored manner, she and her husband Kesari performed penances in order to attract Siva's boons. Eventually he was satisfied by the couple's devotion and caused Vayu to carry a piece of fertility-bringing sacred cake to Anjana, who upon eating it, conceived. As soon as Hanuman was born, Anjana wished to return to Heaven, and so she abandoned her simian son with the words that "fruit as ripe as the morning sun" would provide his food. On seeing the sun rise, Hanuman mistook it for an apple, and his mother's words rang in his ears. Being a child of air, he levitated toward the sun, and swallowed it.

Rahu, bringer of eclipses, was irritated by the interloper on his solar territory and complained to Indra, god of gods. Like Zeus in later Grecian myth, Indra struck the presumptuous underling with a thunderbolt, wounding him and returning him to earth with a thump. The enraged Vayu swept Hanuman away to the furthest reaches of the earth, determined to protect him from further harm. However, a world without wind, or indeed air, cannot function properly for long, and soon the other gods were begging Vayu to return. He agreed, on the understanding that they must each bless little Hanuman with a boon. The accumulation of blessings from so many gods made Hanuman a force to be reckoned with.

Hanuman's early attraction to the sun did not wane. He chose Surya, the solar god, for his guru, and used his superhuman powers to follow the sun's diurnal course in order to attend his lessons. Soon he was as learned in the Vedas as an ancient yogi, and became a close friend of Sugriva, Surya's exiled son, also of simian extraction. They were together when Hanuman first encountered Rama, who was on a quest to look for his abducted wife, Sita. Rama won Hanuman's heart instantly. From that moment on, Hanuman's every word and deed was dedicated to Rama. Devotional images of Hanuman often depict him tearing his chest open in a manner reminiscent of the Christian "sacred heart," to reveal the images of Rama and Sita within. Hanuman is a symbol of devotion perfected.

Hanuman's attempt to eat the sun represents both his early craving for spiritual knowledge and the obfuscating properties of physical and emotional desire, in this case hunger and the need to be nurtured, which hide the light of the spiritual sun behind clouds of Maya illusion. After this early lesson, Hanuman masters all of his senses and slays the "demons" they represent. He is worshipped in consequence as dispeller of wicked and sensuous thoughts.

Despite his loving nature, Hanuman is terrible when roused. In battle he is capable of slaying many-armed powerful demons, which he does with relish. Ravana, abducter of Sita, is, of course, top of his list once he has met Rama. The Ramayana tells the epic adventures of Hanuman and Rama on their mission to rescue Sita, who is held prisoner in Lanka. At one point Hanuman sets the whole city ablaze using his tail as a torch, simultaneously illustrating his courage, ignorance of pain, and his blazing spiritual radiance.

Hanuman is often described as "of golden color," as are many saintly beings. He wears "fine clothes" and "shining earrings," a heroic garb perhaps best paralleled by beautiful Krishna, though seduction could not be further from Hanuman's agenda. While Krishna brings souls to God through ecstatic love, Hanuman brings them through steadfast application to duty, unwavering devotion, and courageous action. He is also famed for his intelligence and tactical skill, and the legend in which he brings a life-giving herb to the dying Lakshmana adds a pharmaceutical aspect to his skills. Recalling this, he wears a sash of sacred devotional grass (known as *kusa grass*). One prayer to Hanuman translates as, "All diseases are destroyed and pains vanish when your powerful name is repeated incessantly (with love and devotion);" the idea being that the mind bathed in the bliss of communion with God (available through Hanuman as intermediary) perceives no bodily pain, which is transient and illusory compared to eternal spiritual truths. Hanuman's position as intermediary is symbolized by his status as gatekeeper to the house of Rama and Sita, whose blessing can heal any complaint.

In a similar psycho-spiritual vein, Sita bestows on Hanuman the ability to grant the "eight powers" (*siddha* skills) and "nine wealths" (types of devotion). The former range from the occult ability to reduce oneself to the size of an atom to the power to subjugate all men. Needless to say, Hanuman is highly proficient in all these skills. One of his favorite techniques is that of *Mahima*, or expanding to an infinitely large size, in order to crush demons.

Hanuman is therefore brave, adaptable, and unwaveringly devoted to the task in hand. He is steadfast in action, gallant, and willing to sacrifice everything in the cause of greater good. Although he is powerful, wealthy, and handsome (his qualities shining through his simian looks), he never abuses his power, but always seeks to put it to good use. He is the perfect role model for those who seek courage in challenging situations, and who require initiative and intelligence in the cause of a higher ideal. He epitomizes the principle of Karma Yoga, or liberation through Right Action.

Contacting Hanuman

A new moon is always a good time to initiate new projects. As the moon waxes, so, too, can your fortunes in the venture augment. However, when the impulse is there, it is always good to follow it up (intelligent discrimination withstanding). Tuesday is traditionally Hanuman's day, so this is the best day to perform your visualization. If you are feeling dynamic and inspired toward a certain cause, particularly if this is philanthropic, Hanuman will be easily accessed.

Visualization for Success in a Tricky Venture

No incense or candles are necessary for this visualization.

Stand at the center of a quiet room, your legs comfortably apart, palms upward, eyes shut.

Envisage Hanuman swinging down into your room in his glowing golden armor, his expression resolute but not devoid of compassion, a quality that emanates from his soft, brown eyes. To his enemies, however, he looks formidable, and you can see within that tender gaze a glint of fierce strength in reserve. This you will use to cut away any obstacles to your philanthropic, or otherwise worthy, venture.

As he jumps off the creeper to which he is clinging, connect your third eye to the monkey god's eye with a vibrant line of light. As you do so, be aware of ageless wisdom and strength being communicated to you through this god who strives, always, to attain perfection, not for his own sake, but through love of God. Feel his sweet breath on your face, the *prana* of inspiration. Fill your lungs with his resolve and ability to avoid or remove all opponents to cosmic progress.

Think very clearly of your exact aim. Visualize it being fulfilled, and then see it being brought into the material realms, as an actuality. Test the "fact" factor: you will instantly perceive whether or not it is viable.

Commune with Hanuman for as long as seems productive; then thank him. When he has swung away on his creeper, return to your room.

As with all visualizations, it is very helpful to write down and interpret your experience. Often events can occur on the plane of such experiences (which I usually term the Astral Plane, especially when the experience is deep and vivid), which seem dreamlike on returning to base, and it can be easy to brush them off as products of an overactive imagination, or just to immediately forget them. Wiccans, of course, will record such experiences in their Book of Shadows—where magickal experiments and encounters are catalogued, interpreted, and developed. One of the main points of such visualizations is to prompt the subconscious and Higher Self into action—or rather, to render their perpetual action tenable to our mundane consciousness—so all events, symbols and "clues" should be carefully mulled over afterward.

A good knowledge of symbolism is essential to such practices. This is best acquired through reading and learning from the myths and legends of all cultures, but a few "shortcuts" are available, such as Frederick Goodman's book *Magic Symbols*, or Aleister Crowley's rather more complex *777*.

Whatever your frame of reference, your intuition should tell you whether the signals you received from Hanuman regarding your endeavour were positive or not. If they seemed negative, it's best to reconsider to your plans. If, however, Hanuman's response seemed enthusiastic, apply yourself with steady effort to the job in hand. If it is in the cause of good, and you fight for your beliefs, you are sure to succeed.

VISUALIZATION FOR LEADERSHIP SKILLS

This visualization is applicable to any situation in which clear thinking and leadership are required, especially those involving group work. Hanuman, chief warrior with his army of monkeys, is adept at synchronizing the efforts of his band to attain maximum efficiency. The same principle may be applied to factory, office, social group, or home.

The qualities we will attain during this visualization are: conviction, confidence, communication skills, cooperation from the group, and finally, action.

The first thing required for efficient leadership is *conviction*. Hollow motives will bring doubtful results. We need to believe, like Hanuman, in the absolute rectitude of our course of action. Hanuman's keynote for this was service; so ask yourself, is this project to the greater good? Will others benefit from its long-term results?

To symbolize his belief shedding light on the darkness of wrong-doing, Hanuman used his own tail as a torch. We do not need to go this far, but it would be helpful to visualize a torch of fire representing your project. The brighter it burns, the more completely will your intended crew be attracted to your leadership. Remember, you are lighting the way for them, showing them the path. Hold the torch high, with strong conviction.

Envisage the people you wish to lead standing around you. This can be done in as much detail as appropriate to you at the time. See yourself light your torch with the strength of your conviction. Be sure to invest it mentally with all of your enthusiasm for the venture. Now, thrust your torch into the air, and visualize the rest of the group looking up to admire it.

The next step is to imagine, with no disrespect to your potential followers, that they have a group mind that requires a leader. Just as Hanuman required an army of capable, obedient soldiers to perform his immaculate Will, so do you require a workforce of willing participants. You want them to admire your torch rather than carry their own at this point, so you need to concentrate on your own *confidence*. Even if your convictions are strong, they will get you nowhere without the belief that you can carry them through successfully.

So, visualize the torch you lit earlier, still above their heads, bursting into radiant light as they gaze admiringly at it. Its flames are unusually bright, its flickerings especially fascinating, almost hypnotic. Strongly visualize your followers looking at it, admiring it, being impressed. As you do so, feel yourself puffing up with confidence. This is a wonderful thing you are doing! Feel the inspiration that comes with a blessed project. Your intuition will be telling you by now whether it is viable or not. With a radiant luminary held high above the heads of your captivated workforce, you cannot fail.

Now, having arrested the attention of your potential army, you need to *communicate* your ideas to them. Hanuman was adept at transferring thoughts into actions, and at synchronizing the efforts of his warriors.

Envisage the torch held aloft, and again, the people you will lead looking at it with captivated interest. They are not so much individuals now, as far as this exercise is concerned, but have a visible mutual focus, that of your torch.

Think of the part you would like each person to play. As you do so, see a flame from the torch extending and penetrating their forehead just between the brows. Only do this if the scheme is ethical; otherwise it will backfire horribly. If it is simply to elicit *cooperation* from a ramshackle group, fine; but never try to make a person act out of character of perform anything you would not be happy being responsible for yourself. The best-case scenario is to infiltrate each individual with light from the torch—shedding light on their consciousness, and thus allowing them to decide for themselves the part they would like to play. If it really is a good idea, you are simply helping them to focus and decide. All of the most successful wars are waged by true believers.

Make sure you use the torch at this point as a light-shedding instrument. See it dispelling the shadows of their doubts and fears, and replacing them with lucidity and confidence.

Next, we need to visualize the group acting in unison to facilitate the plan. For this to come about, they must respect you as well as the project, so, still holding that flaming wand aloft, it is time to concentrate a little on the light-bearer.

Hanuman was respected and obeyed because of his pure motives, always in the cause of higher good; his courage, charisma, and gallantry. It is more fun to follow a hero than a well-meaning dullard, so it is time to enhance your personal image in the eyes of your group.

Still holding the torch of your project, see its light extending down your gold-embroidered sleeve, shining on the jewel-encrusted suit of armor beneath which you stand erect, your spine as straight as your intent. It would be particularly effective to visualize yourself as Hanuman at this point, though his unusual form (for a hero) may provide a mental obstacle for some. In the West, we are not used to perceiving simian traits as especially positive, though by now the reader should have a fairly strong opinion to the contrary. Whether you chose to visualize yourself as the monkey warrior-god, or as your ordinary self enhanced by Hanuman's paraphernalia, feel your bravery, and the fact that you would face opposition without a frisson of fear in this cause. See yourself leading the group to victory, them fighting for you but never doing anything you would not do yourself, or which you could have spared them. It is essential to be gallant, like Hanuman. When others take our lead, it is our responsibility to do our best by them. They are our charges, and if things go wrong through our own unwise counsel, the Karma is all our own. So visualize yourself, holding the torch, shedding light on your admiring, interactive army, an upright leader who encourages graceful action with choreographed precision.

Visualize the "pattern" of your project working itself out before you, appreciate the celestial symmetry that blesses any rightfully inspired scheme. See how the each individual works differently to contribute to the final whole.

The final, finishing ingredient is *action*. Go through the entire process above once more at speed, simply visualizing yourself lighting the torch with your conviction, it flaming up in response to your confidence, reaching out to communicate with the others you wish to involve, then yourself encouraging them to cooperate by being a figure of authority and admiration, the "pattern" of your desired effect, and finally, mentally set the environment—office, factory, meeting hall, or whatever it might be—ablaze with your idea. See it "catching on" like wildfire. See it shedding light where once there was darkness, like Hanuman when he set Lanka ablaze, killing the demons, and rescuing Sita.

You are now ready to present your ideas to those concerned.

MUNDANE ARCHETYPES

The Hanuman-type is intelligent, active, and devoted in service. He innovates but never for the sake of praise; he does it for the greater good and because it is possible.

The hallmark of Hanuman is his practicality. He is adept at organizing schemes and ventures, especially the expeditions he so enjoys, and will expertly coordinate the venture, plot the route, pack the supplies, and then drive the vehicle. He is enthusiastic and capable, an expert leader of the younger or less focused. Others trust him.

His most annoying trait is excessive enthusiasm. When others are not as inspired as he, Hanuman can be quite relentless in his efforts to involve them in this schemes. He is often found attached to a religious organization, to which he feels unbridled, free-flowing loyalty. He is not held there by guilt or fear, but by active pleasure.

TAROT CARDS

Two of Wands, The Magician, The Hierophant

BRAHMA

Darkness. Silence and darkness.

Then, inside its endless vacuum, a pattern different to that of the rest of eternity. A place where atoms stick together, striking up combinations unknown elsewhere, causing motion, friction, and through this, the beginning of the self-created mind of Brahma.

Darkness.

Brahma's thoughts expand like fractals in the blackness, thundering through the ether, causing other things to move around them. Motion starting.

The Brahma-seed conceives a dream—a life-giving liquid, a sea of possibilities. At this fertile thought, the oceans of the world spring up.

Brahma moves his mind across the waters, wishing to dispel the all-pervasive lack of light, to make himself other than Internal. So he sends out a seed, a bright and glowing golden orb to work upon the waters and bring forth life. And then there was Light.

Delirious with success, Brahma emanates excited thought-waves into the ether and over the deep blue and purple seas, moving them, churning them, causing the very first subreactions.

Now externalized, he feels that he is Spirit, and that Outside is matter, and although the two—two!—are joined, they are also different in substance.

He sends out a ray of white light from the lotus at the top of his Being, and he calls it Crown, and as he speaks it, so does it Become. This done, he sends out a ray of violet light from his brow, and as it is received, he called it Ajna. And then Brahma sends out and speaks the rays of blue, and green, and yellow, orange and red, and the constitution of the causal and the astral bodies is complete.

These bodies, one contained within the other, Brahma dresses with flesh, while himself he keeps incorporeal, beholding his creation with four spiritual faces, four points of the skies.

He makes the light and darkness meet in the middle, and causes them to cooperate. And everything he desires, he speaks it, and it Is.

Brahman is the Ultimate Reality, the union of all gods. This word is a great deal older than the name of the god Brahma, and signifies the Priest caste as well as Ultimate God. The aspect of Creator is personified by Brahma, the four-headed god who, along with Vishnu and Siva, forms the Hindu Trinity. Brahma represents the formative, Vishnu the sustaining, and Siva the destructive aspects of Brahman, the Absolute God. His name originally meant "sacred utterance," as the world is believed to have been created through sound. This is why mantras are of such great importance in the Hindu religion; like the Trinity itself, they have the power to create, sustain, and destroy.

Light has similar properties, a fact now recognized in laser science, but used in Hinduism and magick for thousands of years. Light frequencies can enhance or destroy. For one interpretation of their esoteric properties, see Alice Bailey's *Rays and Initiations* (published by Lucis Press).

In the Upanishads, written around 800 B.C.E., Brahma is Atman; that is, both the individual soul and the cosmic self. His power is all-pervasive. He is eternal, like man's spirit, and everything is Brahma, everything is sacred. This is pretty much what Brahman signifies today, while Brahma is a major cult deity with a specific personality, a member of the Hindu family pantheon. As Brahma represents the Vedas, so his wife Sarasvati represents their wisdom and practical application. They combine to produce Ultimate Sagacity.

However, all gods are aspects of Brahman, and thus as with any deity, all lives may be perceived as being lived with and within Brahma. All food and air and sunlight are Brahma, and death is Brahma, as is rebirth.

In Hinduism, we find ourselves perpetually surrounded by, and cradled in, the sacred. This contrasts with the "good" and "bad" dualities of, for example, Christianity. It also makes for a decidedly liberating outlook on life, for nothing is finite, and life itself an illusion, thus ridding us of the need to worry. Emotions are transient. To be under their sway is to be in the grip of Maya, or illusion. It is certainly easier to perceive this all-pervasive divinity in a country in which all is unified and externalized by the heat, than in a cold climate which draws the individual into his own shell and creates a feeling of detachment from the "outside" world. There is a spiritual translucence to the Indian climate which is almost permanent, where in the West, multidimensional areas are fewer and are activated less frequently. This is partly due to the greater consciousness of such principles in India, and partly to do with the abundance of heat coupled with the deprivation of nearly everything else. An underfed populace, much of it living and dying in the street, coupled with an intense religious awareness, produces a degree of spiritual translucence unrivalled in the physically sated, happily housed West. Of course, there are parts of India in which materialism rules the atmospheric roost, just as there are powerful psychic power-points in all other countries, but India exists in closer proximity to the "Universal Subconscious" than any other country I've visited. It is certainly the natural home for an ultimate deity who manifests in all things.

The main bone of contention for the Westerner attempting to embrace the ideas of Hinduism, either on a spiritual or an intellectual basis, is the caste system. How can it be, we may wonder, that a religion that vaunts the unity of all things, is so segregated in its practical applications? The idea is that the system represents proximity to Brahman; thus, it's purported that the Brahmin caste, the highest, is of the closest relation to the Ultimate God, while the lower castes represent a gradual descent into Maya. These "Untouchables" are associated with polluting occupations such as rat catching, or dealing with refuse or human waste. Mahatma Gandhi introduced the name *Harijan,* or "child of God," as an alternative to Untouchable, but old habits die hard, and India is still struggling with the caste system, just as other countries continue to battle with the issues of social class, religion, materialism, and xenophobia.

Brahma is said to have issued from the golden Cosmic Egg. This naturally renders him entirely self-created (or "self-laid"), and allies him with a whole body of mythology concerning such sources of origin. In Hinduism, the most pertinent comparison is with the purple Akashic egg, the symbol of all knowledge, past, present, and future. Obviously the golden egg predates this, as all knowledge springs from Brahman. However, both represent pockets of inestimable futurity, potent capsules of potential. From the golden egg springs creation in its entirety, just like the later Orphic egg of Greek mythology. Other sources locate his origin as a lotus growing in the navel of Vishnu.

Either way, Brahma and his consort Sarasvati are the source of all creation, the origin of time and space, the causal factor or *primum mobile.* Brahma creates the primordial waters first, as does Ra, and lives in them. In this aspect he is known as *Narayana.* He then creates the principle of "Being and Not-Being," i.e., that which is external to him; and then creates the soul and physical vehicles.

The Shakti of Brahma is *Vac* (meaning speech), later known as Sarasvati. The latter is worshipped for the creative intelligence innate in the holy sound "OM" (see *Invoke the Goddess*). All humankind originated from the pair, most notably the wisest and strongest of leaders, who are purported to be direct descendants. Swami Harshananda cites Manu, "the Adam of the Aryan race," as Brahma's great-grandson.

Brahma is depicted with four heads, representing the quarters of the globe. He also peers into each of the four *Yugas*, or eras, aware of the secrets of each and observing the conduct of his creations throughout. Brahma's four faces are said to have arisen when Vac was dancing around him, and he didn't wish to miss a single move. It reminds us that Brahma can look in every direction and every dimension simultaneously. There is no level of reality that cannot be observed by him, and states of linear time—past, present, and future—provide no obstacle to his searing insight. This faculty is very similar to the states approaching Samadhi described by some Indian mystics. For example, Paramahansa Yogananda describes in his *Autobiography of a Yogi* an experience of standing in the street and suddenly being able to see *into* and *beyond* both people and time. Certainly this faculty is reflected in mystical experiences of many religious backgrounds, but in no god is it more accurately depicted than in the many-headed, wise, and peaceful Brahma.

Brahma is usually described as wearing a robe of brilliant white, indicative of his celestial purity, and riding on either a peacock or a swan, both birds of resplendence and royalty, literal in the case of the former, spiritual in the case of the swan.

He has four arms, and carries an array of symbolic paraphernalia; items of devotion, such as a rosary and a bunch of sacred grass; a book indicative of wisdom, learning, and the four Vedas; a pot of primordial water, indicating his creative capacity; and a hand raised in blessing, ready to grant boons when suitably supplicated. Often he carries a lotus or two, and a dish for alms. Unlike many other gods, he does not have a weapon, or at least I have rarely seen him depicted carrying one. On the occasion when he does, it is the discus, representing the wheels of life (both macrocosmically and microcosmically, as the chakras of the physical and psycho-spiritual constitution), and the life-cauterizing weapon of the gods. Being depicted without protective implements may indicate that Brahma is unassailable.

CONTACTING BRAHMA

Brahma is pleased by austerities, so performing one or two before broaching him will help, for example, abstinence from tobacco, alcohol, or other indulgences. It will also be beneficial to chant a suitable mantra such as, "OM Namo Brahmayaya," which means, more or less, "Prostrations to Lord Brahma."

Face north for this meditation; Brahma's altars are found in the north wall of the temples.

VISUALIZATION FOR LOOKING AT A SITUATION FROM MANY ANGLES

This visualization is particularly good for those people with staunch, possibly entrenched, ideas. These may be political, religious, personal, or any other; they may be borne of individual experience, or imposed by parents, peers, or cultural background, but they are never what we "really think" until we have tried the alternatives.

I was horrified while watching a documentary recently on voting habits among those in their early twenties, to hear a young woman state categorically that she would vote for the Conservative party even if the opposition offered to represent everything she believed in. When asked why, she answered: "Because my parents have always voted Conservative."

So much for the suffragettes! Most of us, hopefully, are more intelligent than this, but just how entrenched are our views? They key to life is flexibility, adaptability, and active intelligence. If you find that you habitually look at something from a particular angle, this visualization is for you. As Alice Bailey put it, "To me, the ultimate hell . . . would be a state of complete satisfaction with one's own viewpoint and therefore such a static condition that all evolution in thought and all progress would be permanently arrested." Sticking to one's guns mindlessly is anti-evolution. It goes against everything we are designed and inclined to facilitate.

Even if you are reasonably open-minded, there are times when it is difficult to get a clear perspective on a situation. It may be too subjective, making it difficult to dissociate emotionally, or you may have been trained into particular responses from birth. With any of these situations, this method should help.

Take several breaths of cleansing white light. Try to visualize your negativity and preconceptions exiting your bodies, physical, emotional, and spiritual, as you exhale, and inhale only objectivity and clarity. Will your mind and responses to be pure.

Now, visualize the experience you wish to interpret from a new angle or two. Imagine it being played out below you. I say below, because you are going to interpret it from a great height, in the form of four-headed Brahma.

At first you find that you are still involved with it, seeing it as pretty much life-size, or possibly even larger than life. But then, with the white light you've been inhaling, you find yourself shooting up, like a fast-growing beanstalk, up and up into the clouds, leaving your situation in miniature below you. From this perspective, you realize how Lilliputian it is, though it seems incredibly important when you're in it.

Talking of perspective, it suddenly seems to you as if you have none; or rather, as if you can see everything from every angle. As you look out over the sky and landscape, you realize you are looking in every direction simultaneously. Like Brahma, you have four heads, one looking in each direction, and four sets of eyes.

First, we are going to look at your situation though the eyes of the head facing north. This is the nearest equivalent to your everyday point of view. However, it is infinitely loftier.

Open your "northern" pair of eyes and contemplate the situation beneath you. Pick out particular characters and think about what it is that you either defend or attack about them. What do they do to deserve this?

When you are ready, close that viewpoint and open the eastern one. Now you see the same scene, drenched in a sunrise. There is an ethereal glow to what had previously seemed a very solid, definite situation; the figures seem almost to entice pathos in you. They are just humans, like all the rest of us, fighting their corner, standing up for what they believe for a brief moment, until we are all gone again. From this perspective, all consciousness, however convoluted, seems a mere flash.

This perceived, you are ready to move onto the southern vantage point. As you open this pair of eyes, you are surprised to behold that the gentle glow of dawn has intensified into a fire of passion in the midst of your scene. Look into it and try to relate to the individual calling of each of the players. Go through them one by one. This may be rather exhausting, but will be well worth it for the insights it will bring. One thing you will definitely learn is that there are no 100 percent "rights" or "wrongs" in any given situation. Once everybody's motivations (in bad situations, usually innate misery) are understood, it becomes impossible to be judgmental. We might have opinions, and express them, but that is just what they are—opinions. And yes, there are abusive situations that are clearly immoral, but it can be all too easy to lose touch with the cause and become carried away with the group mindset—a very dangerous thing under such circumstances. Like Brahma, we need to learn to understand all things from all angles, and be intelligent and discriminating in our analyses.

When you have thoroughly empathized with each of the players in your theater of circumstance, you may close your inner eyes on that perspective.

Finally, we have the Western vantage point. You as Brahma open your green eyes to behold water. Water everywhere—a veritable flood. A river of tears. A sea of dissolution.

What has happened to your little set of circumstances and prejudices? Each player is clinging to the nearest piece of driftwood. Some are beginning to sink. They are going back into the primordial ocean, back to the melting place, to be assimilated, reformulated, and brought to life again, in completely different circumstances.

One-by-one, your players meet their inevitable end, just as you will. All of your preciously harbored and presented thoughts, the things you think define you, will dissolve to nothing, as will this civilization, eventually.

As you think this, the final few players sink, a few bubbles temporarily marking their watery graves. These are the only epitaphs any of us can expect; the transient sign of a life one lived, soon joining a greater body.

You feel yourself sinking too. It is not a panic-inspiring feeling, but rather one of repose, like drifting down in a floatation tank, still able to breathe, and equally able to observe the underwater life. Down here may be seen the ancient Egyptian Empire in all its glory; comprised of intricate thought-processes and countless individual sensations and lives lost and now, anonymous. The larger issues remain, rendered immortal by their echo in every human soul; the theme of the afterlife which characterizes this society. The Egyptians knew how to think in perspective. So, of course, do the philosophers of India, which is why we are here.

Beside Egypt lies ancient Greece, many of whose thoughts and entertainments are still available to us today. Looking around, you behold all the lost empires from Rome to Atlantis, the trivial details petrified or washed away, the big structures remaining. Temples, mostly, the product of perspective; and theaters, more often than not, borne of the desire to give it. Watching another life played out on the stage, screen, or in a biography, is a millenia-old technique for taking the human mind out of its prison of individual flesh.

Look around at the aquatic antiquities for as long as you wish. If you have not gained some perspective by now, you never will.

When you are ready, float to the surface of the sea of tears, return to your Brahma stature, and finally diminish yourself slowly back into your human form—physically only, though. Endeavor to keep your multi-angled perspective with you at all times. It will make you a far more meaningful person during this brief span on earth.

Visualization for a Higher Purpose or Attaining a Spiritual Overview

The idea of this meditation is to align your three bodies—the physical (including your day-to-day persona), emotional (astral), and spiritual (body of light; can be accessed through the Higher Self). It is commonly accepted in occultism that when these three "vehicles" are aligned, greater energies are enabled to enter the system, and the incarnation's higher purpose may be recognized and followed.

In the normal course of things, without the aid of meditation and magickal work, these bodies are rarely synchronous, and the life's greater purpose can go ignored. Sudden bursts of inspiration, the strength and insight brought about by a crisis (such as an accident), or a humanitarian calling (helping with a war effort, for example) are usually the only channels for the greater energies to filter through. The "funnel" through which they pour into the crown chakra is narrowed by concentration on the trivial and widened by contemplating the greater picture, and by meditation, magickal work and heartfelt philanthropic action. This visualization will make the downpouring of these energies easier, enabling the subject to perceive the point of their present incarnation. Of course, the more often you perform this exercise, the more effective it will be.

Sit cross-legged (or in lotus posture), facing north. Take several deep breaths of brilliant blue light, allowing the inhalation to glow in your lungs and infiltrate your blood, so soon you are able to perceive your entire body glowing with this bright prana.

Envisage Brahma standing before you, his four crowned heads facing the four quarters, his serene smile of all-pervading wisdom, the bright pink lotus flowers he holds aloft, the hand raised in blessing. He is fluent in every level of existence, a denizen of all dimensions, never captured by the trivial or transient.

On the forehead facing you is a red U-shape, and in the middle of it, the hidden Ajna chakra, or third eye center. Connect your own to his with a line of blue light.

Now, visualize a giant funnel at the top of your skull, its point down, the top growing ever wider in the swirling cosmic energies. Be aware of this as your spiritual recharge point. Do not forget, your body is like a battery which, were it not recharged nightly during sleep, when it relaxes enough to allow these life-energies in, would be very short-lived indeed. Yogis and magickians deliberately acquire large amounts of this energy in order to use the "superfluous" portion for metaphysical purposes. You are going to use yours to "straighten out" your three bodies and allow your true life purpose access to your basic modes of operation. It is essential to carry the spiritual impulse into the physical plane, as every successful practitioner of good magick knows.

Feel your bodies aligning themselves as the influx of bright, positive energy becomes greater. A cloak of white and blue light seems to envelop you, moulding your bodies into one perfected vehicle of dazzling white light.

When you are satisfied that you have imbibed as much energy as you are able, and that your three bodies seem to be aligned, you may stop.

Thank Brahma, withdraw the cord of light if you wish, and sit in quiet contemplation for a while.

You may not instantly perceive the answer to your quest; but if you repeat this exercise, the more the better; success is guaranteed. The revelation of your purpose here may of course completely disrupt your present lifestyle, but nothing can be more important than doing what we are here to do, so long as it is in the cause of good. It is up to you, of course, to decide whether to follow the dictate of your Higher Self or not. However, it might be pointed out that the time has never been better to follow your heart. One of the key facts of the Aquarian Age is that doing what you love, and what is positive for others, will bring great rewards on at least one, and possibly all of the levels.

Mundane Archetypes

An archetype that was wholly Brahma would be formidable indeed; usually he is witnessed as an aspect, along with many more "human" traits.

Flashes of intense creative inspiration signify this godform; his archetype displays profound genius in both science and the arts. He might study submolecular physics and then relate it to the formation of the Greek pantheon, drawing mind-shattering conclusions from the parallels. He may study the significance of sound on the human body and spirit, experimenting with harmonies and cacophonies, or break new ground with light frequencies and geo-cosmological codices.

There is much of the "mad professor in the basement" in the Brahma archetype. He is unlikely to meet with any convention, while causing orthodox science and education to include him by blowing their minds with innovative truths.

Without genius, Brahma vanishes.

Tarot cards

The World, The Moon, The Tower, Death

EGYPTIAN GODS

THOTH

A crescent moon upon my forehead, I sit beneath the sands and bark like a baboon. Blue light swoons into me, carrying stars in its vortices; from these I measure the length of the cosmic days and nights, and prophecy implodes in my mind, pulsars of truth that the gods allow me to comprehend. Thoth, my god, scholar, scribe, magickian, gives me the wisdom to interpret these signs.

The moon is rich in portent, and though I cannot be eye-to-eye with her down here, I can sense her tides pulling at my eternal soul.

I can make my spirit exit my chimerical priest's body and fly like the ibis to moon-reflecting waters, in which I behold the whiteness of the feathers of my soul, as white as Maat's, weigher of the hearts of men. I look up and see two sister kites span the sky, searching, and I understand Isian tides and how these will affect the mortal realm. I breathe the musty incensed air of the sacred vault, and my spirit flies in liberation on fresher breezes, a god's-eye view of human life below.

I am the servitor of Thoth, blessed by his powers of prophecy, interpretation, philosophy. All knowledge is his, all sacred and secular understanding. Under the light of his lamp I work, translating his holy hieroglyphs, that men might understand. The result is every helpful tome, every grimoire, every book of shadows known to the world.

In all forms of divination I abide, bringing celestial symmetry closer to human interpretation.

Thoth is represented by the moon, and in respect of its lunar color, by the ibis bird. Sometimes, like Siva and Horus, he is depicted with the moon as his left eye and the sun as his right, reflecting cosmic balance. As a god of wisdom and knowledge, this befits him.

Thoth created eight elemental deities, the *Ogdoad,* four of whom were female with the heads of serpents, and four male, with frog heads. Keket and Kek were darkness, Nunet and Nun were the ocean, Hehet and Theh were boundless space, and Amunet and Amun the power of invisibility—probably springing from the idea of the primordial invisible force, the wind. These in turn perpetuated existence through the sounds of their own voices. They were known also as the "souls of Thoth," and sang and chanted to keep the sun rotating and the sky from falling.

In the same manner as in Hindu creation myth, Thoth is purported to have created the Universe through the faculty of sound. This gives us an important clue regarding a dimension of Egyptian magick that is not recorded; the relevance of the rhythm and pitch of the incantations, prayers, and spells that accompanied the amply illustrated Egyptian sacred ritual. It has long been recognized in the science of magick, of which Thoth is a patron, that sound has the power to create and destroy on all levels: physical, etheric, and spiritual. That the ancient Egyptians were aware of this there can be no doubt; and though their religious ceremony was spectacularly visual, involving an immense amount of creative visualization, we may deduce with confidence that it was also very carefully structured on an aural level, like a Hindu ritual.

Thoth, like Brahma, is associated with the primordial Cosmic Egg, underlining this creative faculty. Both gods split one shell (or reality level) to reveal the creative potential of the hidden reality within. This in turn develops its own shell (the flesh of Maya, or illusion), and thus the Cosmic Egg forever retreats within, waiting for a god to extract it and again reveal the new realities of inner consciousness. In the same way does the self-begotten Thoth and Brahma seek to release the innate spiritual consciousness of mankind.

Although Thoth has been extensively linked with the Greek god Hermes, in several ways his functions are more akin to those of Apollo. He is intimately associated with the art of prophecy, and like Apollo's *Pythias,* Thoth's priests would sit in caves and underground temples delivering answers to a divination-hungry populace. Thoth is variously referred to as the "tongue" of Ra and Ptah, emphasizing his role as divine channel. Sometimes his priests would wear ape masks, reflecting Thoth's chimerical connection with the baboon; at other times an actual ape would provide, through its erratic barking, the answers sought by the supplicant. The servitor of Thoth would then interpret the message.

A natural progression from the spoken sound is the written word, and Thoth the scribe is said to have invented hieroglyphs, known as "the words of the gods," encapsulating the essence of Maat, sacred Truth. As in other religions in which it is believed that the word has the power to manifest its import on the physical (and always on the etheric and spiritual) planes, the faculty of sound and meaning are a sacred commodity to the ancient Egyptian. To misuse the word would be sacrilege, and a dangerous one at that. We may safely guess that the sacerdotal caste kept its hieroglyphs and incantations well concealed from the bulk of the populace.

One of the aspects of existence controlled and measured by Thoth is Time itself. He is said to have divided the expanse of time into aeons, centuries, and finally years, and to have devised the three seasons, twelve months of the year, and the three ten-day weeks that fitted into each. This role certainly befits a deity with solar, and particularly lunar, correspondences. Seshat, a stellar goddess and Thoth's female equivalent (sometimes said to be his wife), is similarly linked with the written and spoken word, and the art of measurement. Seshat was a deity particular to the Pharaoh, and was variously known as "mistress of the house of books," reflecting her Thoth-like aspects, and "mistress of the house of architects," demonstrating her mathematical exactitude, basis of firm foundations both physical and metaphysical, and the protective aspect she evinces for Pharaoh and kingdom alike. She is associated with exactitude, calculation, and list-making, all of which are organizational skills essential to efficiently running a domain. Like Thoth, Seshat is linked with archive-making and history; that is, the important art of recording and learning from past action. Both deities are intimately connected with practical as well as theoretical magick.

Egyptian priests claimed metaphorical use of Thoth's library; one can only imagine the wonders that a primordial magickian's grimoires might contain. Tarot cards, thought in occult lore to have to come to Europe from India via Egypt, are often referred to as the "Lost Book of Thoth." The Major Arcana represent stages of initiation, while the four suits of the Minor Arcana signify processes of development, of control over the elements that constitute the human condition. Thoth presides over all of these stages, from the apparent mundanity of the suit of Pentacles to the most elevated initiation symbolized by the World card. Every footstep, however seemingly dull, is of significance in one's overall progress, and the neophyte and initiate alike will recognize this.

All metaphysical knowledge stems from the source of the divine magickian's wisdom, and the Akashic records are another name for the Library of Thoth. Many European magickal tracts, particularly from medieval and Elizabethan times, are attributed to "Hermes Tristmegistus," the "thrice-great Hermes" who devolved from the legend of Thoth via ancient Greece and its association with Hermes. The cap of invisibility worn by his Greek counterpart recalls Thoth, and both might be connected with sleep and illusion, but there seems little else to convincingly connect the great Egyptian master of magick with the Olympian messenger, trickster, and god of thieves.

Thoth is said to have helped Isis perform the resurrection of Osiris by lending his "true" voice to her spells, and to have caused Osiris to become victorious over Seth in the House of Ra. This is a civilizing quality, as Seth represents among other things the cannibalistic urge, while Osiris signifies agriculture, growing crops to alleviate the need to eat human flesh.

As infallible scribe, Thoth was able to record and proclaim the truth at the celestial tribunal between Seth, Osiris, and Horus. Thoth is frequently mentioned in the Book of the Dead in this capacity, in the hope that he will favor the new "Osiris," the spirit of the recently deceased, with a similar victory over death. Thoth is continually invoked to aid the destruction of foes and situations of enmity.

Isis was tutored in magick by Ra and Thoth, the latter of whom shielded the infant Horus from pestilence and the negative energies of his cruel uncle Seth. Thoth provided antidotes to those diseases besetting Horus, and frequently displayed the traits of a divine apothecary, reflecting his lunar associations through the science of plant and herb use, and the all-important timing of ritual workings. He rescued the eyes of both Ra and Horus, the latter having lost one during a battle with Seth who had shapeshifted into the form of a black pig.

Another of Thoth's wives is Maat, the goddess of absolute moral rectitude and spiritual integrity (see *Invoke the Goddess*). In the "Hymn to Ra," which appears at the beginning of the Book of the Dead, their joint connection with right timing is echoed: "The god Thoth and the goddess Maat have written down [thy course] for thee daily and every day." They do not necessarily decide the measure of a man's life, as do the Greek Fates or Norse Norns, but they accurately assess it and once it is recorded, it is indelible. Thus they are heavily linked to the idea of pre-destination, explaining in part Thoth's connection with prophecy. Thoth is depicted witnessing the Judgment of the Dead in order to record the result of the ritual weighing of the heart, the opposite pan of the scales containing Maat's feather of truth. Occasionally, the Pillar of Balance on which the scales rest is surmounted by Thoth's head, recalling one of his most pertinent symbols, the similarly shaped palm measure by whose notches calculations are made.

Another important function of Thoth was as purifier. He helped Isis cleanse Osiris' slain body of Seth's dark spells, which was necessary to aid Osiris' resurrection. He presided over royal ritual cleansing, aiding the future Pharaoh, the span of whose life and reign he had already recorded at conception, with his vivifying lustral bath.

The festival of Thoth was celebrated in the eponymous month, on the nineteenth day, following the full moon, which marked the beginning of the year.

Thoth is depicted as a dog-headed baboon, often with a crescent or full moon on his forehead. Sometimes he wears a headdress similar to that worn on occasion by Sekhmet, characterized by a figure of eight, from which rays of light and heat are emitted. This shape, symbolic of eternity, is well-known for its healing powers and the ability to combat linear time, an essential tool for any magickian. This means maintaining a flexible consciousness. "Linear time" is created by a primary belief in the physical, and giving this more weight (literally) than the winged mind and soul (the *Ka* and *Ba* so easily recognized by the Egyptians).

Occasionally Thoth is represented as a mummy, underlining his connection with funeral rights, immortality, and the realms of the dead. It is Thoth who as scribe records, and thus renders eternal, the verdict passed in the Hall of Assessors. He transfers the cosmic into the tenable—and thus irrevocable. The power of the word, both spoken and written, cannot be overestimated in Egyptian magick. (See the Brahma chapter for more on this.)

CONTACTING THOTH

The best time of the month to communicate with Thoth is at the full moon.

A purifying bath with psychically enhanced salts will put you in the right frame of mind. Dead Sea salt crystals, widely available from pharmacies and toiletry stores, are easy and aesthetically pleasing to use in magickal baths. However, a fistful of table salt will work just as well. The essential point is to visualize it cleansing your bodies, and then it will.

Candles and a special robe may help you attune to this Master of Ceremonial Magick.

Incense should be thick and sweet. Select one that sets you in a mystical frame of mind. (I usually find that *Dark Musk* joss-sticks by Spiritual Sky do the trick.)

VISUALIZATION FOR POWERS OF DIVINATION

In my experience, by far the most effective form of divination is the Tarot. However, horses for courses, and if you prefer Runes, alternative divination decks, or even the good old tea leaves, fair enough. It is of course not the objects that do the work, but our intuition working off the clues given.

They may be psychological props, but the results gained from a trusty pack of Tarot can be astonishing. If you do not already possess a set, I wholeheartedly recommend the Rider-Waite, which are easy to learn and replete with useful magickal correspondences. My other personal favorite is the *Tarot of the Old Path* by Howard Rodway (available from Element Books in the UK), a beautifully rendered Wiccan pack. However, the most important thing is to feel personally attracted to the pack, so chose the one your intuition tells you is right for you.

Light seven candles of silver, blue, and white. Place your tools of divination in the direct light of the silver candle.

Imagine Thoth sitting opposite you, in whatever form you prefer—as a man, a baboon, or an ibis chimera. In all cases he wears a moon disc on his forehead and emanates a silver-purple light. His edges shimmer. Bizarre mental equations come into your mind as you look at him.

Concentrate on your third eye area, bathing it in purple light. Now coagulate this light into a powerful ray and send it into the center of your divination equipment.

As you do so, Thoth does the same. With the impact of his concentrated energy, visualize your tools or cards almost levitating with this very refined, intelligent, arcane energy. See how something about them—their aura—seems to reorganize itself, expanding, reshuffling atomically.

As with all of these exercises, more may occur that is impossible to predict. If Thoth has a special message for you, you will receive it now. This is may be concerned with educational issues, magickal practice, or your future. These are certainly ideal areas about which to enquire with your Thoth-enhanced divination equipment.

When you are both ready, thank Thoth, and close the contact by withdrawing the line of light and saying "So mote it Be."

A divination performed immediately after this exercise should prove highly effective. When using your cards/stones/crystal in future, visualize them surrounded by Thoth's light, possibly even held in his hands as you shuffle/shake/scrutinize. This will enhance your ability to interpret the symbols, which are the Cosmic Intelligence's way of communicating with us.

VISUALIZATION FOR RECALLING LIFE'S INNER MYSTERY

Daily life is by its very nature mundane; with all the trivial things we have to do, appointments to keep, work to perform, it can be easy for even the most magickally minded person to forget the more interesting and meaningful side of existence. Thoth, as Lord of Wisdom and Magick, is well placed to jolt our memories to life's higher, deeper purpose.

The candle and incense specifications for this visualization are the same as the previous exercise.

Take several deep, slow breaths of blue and silver light, and imagine these colors infiltrating your bodies as you do so. Very gently, feel a sense of relief being absorbed into you as your mind becomes freer to wonder. Realize how fettered it has been by small concerns, worthless in the long term.

You begin to perceive a sensation of your consciousness "peeling away" from your body, an experience which brings a sense of levity and otherworldliness. Yet it is somehow more real and more permanent than the trivial, emotional consciousness you harbored before.

Now you find yourself in a hot land at night. There is no light, just warm dust underfoot and the heat emanating from pyramids all around, which are not visible, but you know they are there. Glyphs of consciousness hang in the ancient air, invisibly emanating a sense of arcane hierarchy and purpose. Mages have meditated here, magickians have walked in ritual procession muttering mantras of geometric precision, and many a soul has navigated these labyrinths in the quest for stellar immortality.

The only light, indeed, comes from the stars, the constellations extra-luminous tonight, no stretch of the imagination as they seemed before. Now the patterns are obvious—the tunic of Orion, where Osiris comes from; the dog-star Sothis, heralding the Lady Isis; a map for spirits seeking union with the eternal.

Looking back to ground level, you see before you a cave, the inside cast in thick shadows like a magickian's velvet cape, the mouth faintly starlit, just enough to define it for you.

You peer inside, but the darkness thickens like a curtain. What you do perceive, however, is the muffled sound of a chant coming from, it seems, the most chthonic recesses of the deep, black cave.

Cautiously, you step inside. Edging forward one toe at a time, you feel, rather than the expected fear, a sense of awe and excitement, a frisson that passes right thorough you and reminds you of the excitement you felt as a child when a story had reached a potential climax. Inside, the cave smells of cloves and spices.

The mantric music gets louder, and as you approach its source, quite fearlessly, you notice a new and brighter light. One half of the cave is lit in silver-white light, the other in the golden rays of a Mediterranean midday.

The sounds and light and intense rich scents become almost overwhelming as you reach the final recess.

Looking in, you see a very tall man wearing the mask of an ibis bird, its long thin beak protruding conspicuously, and nothing else but a white tunic and exquisitely wrought belt and neckpiece of silver. The sensation of magick and sorcery is so strong in here that you feel that whatever you think or desire will materialize instantly.

"There is nothing unique in this," booms a voice as you stand riveted at the door. "One simply has to go a little further back to find it."

This side of Thoth's profile emits silver light, and as you gaze into it, it begins to seem like moonshine on water, rippling out patterns and mandalas of consciousness, each atom affecting the other, this silver water between everything, so that all is connected.

On his arm alone is a whole ocean of consciousness; you can see your thoughts dropping into it like pebbles, causing ripples that, somewhere, will contribute to waves.

He turns the golden side toward you, and there, in what seems like visible air on his other arm, you see pictures of sparks inside bodies, the bodies ranging from infancy to decrepitude, like a Hare Krishna picture, each with a glowing consciousness. The body becomes a skeleton, the spark detaches, then it descends again on an embryo, and the cycle repeats itself. Wave after wave of flesh breaking on the shores of the mundane, containing the divine consciousness, all too often forgetting it, thus necessitating another round on the wheel of dualities.

As you think this, Thoth, still chanting, turns to face you. One eye blazes gold, the sun; the other shines in silver. Neither is outdone or compromised by the other. Both are in perfect unity.

The light from each luminary is interweaving itself down a staff held by Thoth at his beak; the staff becomes a caduceus, half the interweaving light solar and half lunar. He hands it to you.

As you receive the staff, be totally aware of your true descent, nothing to do with genes and physical inheritance, but a trip down from the stars to inhabit the temporary vehicle that will best enable you to learn the intended lessons of this incarnation.

"Look for signs and symbols," intones the stentorian Thoth, "for this is how we guide you. Every situation, every chance encounter, every thing you see *when your intuition is activated* is there to signal your route."

Does this include what number bus you catch, or who's sitting beside you in a restaurant? you wonder incredulously. Thoth catches you with his resplendent eyes.

"Not always, but when the time is right. Meditation facilitates it, as does magick. No need to be semiotically aroused all the time, or others will doubt and discredit you. Recall the basic precepts of magick—to Know, to Will, to Dare, and to be Silent. Speak only to others who understand you. Those who do not will only drag you into their own low vibrations, and an experience of this type shared is an experience halved. Use your own language, be unique. We can speak to you more clearly this way. Invent your alphabet of symbols, ask us to communicate with you, and it will become possible."

Needless to say, now is the time to discuss any other issues you may have brought into this visualization. Thoth is so measured and in control that it is easy to stay as long as you wish. He is rather like a very friendly, informal doctor and teacher rolled into one, the bizarre appearance notwithstanding.

When you are ready, simply thank Thoth, and with a wave of the caduceus, return yourself to your room.

Daily meditation and magickal activity will keep you on this wavelength most of the time. However, it is worth noting that the so-called "mundane" is also important, especially when perceived in its symbolic aspect—and that all of the best masters and magickians have a foot planted in both worlds. They are never proud or haughty about their spiritual achievements, as the wise person knows how much further there still is to go. Not until we are reabsorbed back into the Creative Intelligence in a pure and eternal state have we really reached the goal.

MUNDANE ARCHETYPES

The mundane archetype of Thoth is nearly always a man of forty or older. He wears black suits or other striking apparel—a poignant talisman, perhaps—and emanates a sense of serious learning combined with many years' practical experience. He is often a High Magickian or Qabalist.

Thoth is an arresting, organized teacher. His sinister aspect may, however, prove unnerving. A partial Thoth archetype may become the egotistical occult guru we all know and hate (once the scales have fallen from our eyes): manipulative and intent on using his psychological and magickal prowess for all the wrong ends. However, the Thoth-character, with his integrity still intact, will take his initiate through the grades with every attention to their well-being. He is characterized by lack of selfish interest in his charge, and an uncloying attitude. The really fine incarnate specimen of Thoth will not socialize with those he is teaching, for fear of influencing either himself or them through subjective ephemera. He has his eyes set on far greater, longer-lasting goals.

TAROT CARDS
The Magician, The Moon, The Hierophant

KHEPHRI

I am Khephri in the morning, Ra at midday, and Atum in the evening.

From nothing I rise, heralding new life.

Out of the regions of darkness and waste I forge a future, gathering my strength and shining it onto those who are my supplicants, and all others besides. I do not discriminate, though I can show favor. I protect those who ask me to, both in this life and the next, from all evil influences.

I need not go on; I am a fact that requires no embellishment.

I give and protect and renew the creative source on a diurnal basis.

You could say, I am Life.

Khephri is the scarab ubiquitous in Egyptian sacred painting and talismanic jewelry. The scarab beetle was believed to be, like Thoth, self-created, emerging from dung with no apparent parentage. This may seem an unpleasant and polluting origin to the hygiene-conscious modern mind, but in a hot land wholly dependent on agriculture, the good compost of dung would not be scorned, and the effect of heat would have an overall purifying effect. The emergence of life from waste matter is integral to organic existence, and indicates positive forces at work. The beetle was lucky, and its apotheosis, Khephri, was a powerfully positive and protective force. The connection with the sun gods is obvious; the sacred beetle is, in effect, the son of the sun, Atum, Ra, or Osiris. Khephri often represented the rising sun thanks to the imaginative analogy, mentioned by both Pliny and Plutarch in their writings on Egyptian custom and belief, between the way the scarab beetle rolls a ball of dung before it and the idea of the sun being "pushed" into and along the sky.

Khephri's name means "he who comes into existence," owing to the belief that all scarab beetles were male, and the insect's subsequent appearance of self-renewal. The verb *khepher* also means "to believe," reflecting the idea that the beetle, because apparently born of its own matter, could replicate itself through self-belief, an important point in a magickal context.

Khephri's emergence from the womb of Nut represents the morning sun's emergence from the "underworld" of night, and the colors of dawn associated with birth gave Khephri an additional role as symbol of resurrection of the soul after death, with concomitant associations. The dead were buried heavily decorated with the sigil of perpetually renewed Khephri. Some exquisite examples of the scarab as talisman were unearthed among the jewelry found in the tomb of Tutankhamen.

The pupae of *Scarabaeus sacer* have been said to resemble the dressed mummy, deepening the beetle's symbolic connection with the rites of the dead. The "heart scarab" was one of the most important features of a tomb, as it replaced the heart if the latter had been damaged. This heart-sized, beetle-shaped stone was inscribed more often than not with the thirtieth text of the Book of the Dead:

> *O my heart, which I had from my mother, O my heart, which I had upon earth, do not rise up against me as a witness in the presence of the Lord of Things; do not speak against me concerning what I have done, do not bring up against me anything I have done in the presence of the Lord of the West.*

This incantation is essentially a plea to the conscience of the dead to remain unperturbed during the inquisition in the Hall of the Assessors. It is an interesting feature of the Egyptian state of purity that the trick is not so much to have avoided doing wrong, but to avoid being *perceived* as having done wrong. Historical events were also recorded on the heart scarabs, particularly those belonging to kings and the rulers of *nomes*, or districts. An empire-enhancing enterprise or the urge for battle would therefore be represented in a positive rather than realistic light; for, of course, the gods were Egyptian and keen to expand the domain of their worship, rather than to protect individual rights.

Because of his associations with dawn, Khephri is also identified with "Horus of the horizon," also known as *Harmakhis*. He is often winged like the falcon-headed god. As *Khepher-Ankh*, he appears on papyri pushing a ball of sand fertile with his own seed into the eastern horizon of the sky (see the *Book Am-Tuat*).

Khephri also manifests as a serpent, with a head and a pair of human legs at either end of his body, one facing northwest, the other southeast. The legs face in opposite directions, so that he rotates as he moves, as does the sun. Khephri appears in this manner in the *Book of Gates*, guarding the barque of Ra as it sails its diurnal course. In a more frequent and recognizable form, he appears as a beetle above the neck, and a man from the neck down.

Khephri is a powerfully positive force because he is born daily, and is thus in a state of almost perpetual purity. His regenerative powers represent humanity's hopes—both for rebirth in the afterlife and for "new leaves" in the present. His essential message is alchemical; that dross can be transformed into the gold of potential. The second is that it is never too late to begin anew. All that is required is self-belief and willpower.

Because these properties are propitious to growth, the symbols of Khephri are talismanic. The scarab-beetle was one of the most popular icons of Egypt, used in the household to bring luck and prosperity, about the person for protection, and in the sarcophagus to ensure a blessed afterlife. Here they were to be found at the throat area, often as exquisite glazed amulets, protecting the entire body.

Contacting Khephri

The morning is the only time to access Khephri. For obvious reasons, dawn is best.

Incense should be thick and resinous; loose incense is definitely preferable to joss-sticks. Remember that, with Khephri, life springs from the combination of parching heat and compost, a formula that can be reflected (if not directly imitated!) by your loose incense on its charcoal disc.

Candles should be black, orange, and red. If you are doing the visualization to "turn over a new leaf," a green candle may be added to represent your fresh approach to life.

Visualization for Protection

Once you have lit your candles and loose incense (no bath is necessary; Khephri's origins are barely hygienic!), stand with your eyes closed and fill your body with whitish-blue light. You can do this by deeply breathing in and out as many times as you wish, until it is easy to visualize your body surrounded and infiltrated by this protective light.

Now imagine yourself armored against all ills, encased in a beetle's impenetrable jacket. So safe are you inside this jacket that even the most fearsome, scorching temperatures cannot bake you, or, indeed, cause you discomfort. You are invulnerable inside this coat of protection.

Now visualize every point of your body deflecting attack of any sort. The latter may be represented by bolts of black light, flying arrows, or whatever seems appropriate to you. See the unwanted influences and damaging energies bouncing off your feet, your heels, the backs of your legs, the front, and so on all the way up your body. It is worth taking the time to cover every inch of your bodies, especially if you are under "attack" in the present. If you are male, pay particular attention to your feet, heels, and calves. These are, mythologically, the most vulnerable areas. Also, pay attention to the throat and the delicate area behind the ears. See this negative energy bouncing off every part of your beetle-like armor and returning to sender.

Do not forget to cover your back, the top of your head, and the soles of your feet.

When you have established this coat of astral body armor in your mind's eye, "harden" it with willpower. Say:

> *I am protected by my own power. No evil will penetrate me here. I am invulnerable to attack.*

Mentally reconfirm the fortitude of your astral armor, and the fact that it will stay with you, insuperable.

Renewing it every morning will work wonders. Make sure that you do so, if under psychic, psychological, or physical attack. The moment at dawn has the most power to endow your astral armor.

VISUALIZATION FOR TURNING OVER A NEW LEAF

This exercise is particularly relevant to those who find themselves regularly, particularly daily, confronted with self-inflicted urges that are difficult to overcome.

Your present situation may be visualized as a pile of dung. Not a pleasant image, but neither are the habits and experiences you wish to kick.

Take a deep breath and imagine the clean life-force in the cosmos glowing in your lungs and spreading outward. Know that life goes on and that it is never too late to change. Breathe this conviction in and out steadily—do not hyperventilate—just take slightly deeper, more aware breaths than you usually take.

Despite this new infiltration of purity, you are still sitting here in your heap of self-created psychic excreta. Any repeated and unwanted habit creates this unwholesome aura, and the toxicity of it can cause the cycle to repeat itself simply because it is familiar. You may feel "better the Devil you know"; you may seek subterfuge in this much-repeated action, but in truth, you are enslaved by it.

Visualize a vibrant red-gold sun in the air before you. This represents the new circumstances you wish to attain. The heat radiating from this beautiful, spiritual sphere is strong enough to burn all of the filthy cords that connect you to the habits you wish to break. Feel it on your face, your neck, arms, and back. Feel it scorching the dung heap surrounding you, turning the latter to inoffensive dust.

You must be resolute in your decision. The alternative? A trip down the psychic plug-hole, into the abyss. You know that you need to change; otherwise you would not be reading this.

Concentrate on the spiritual sun, which shines with the potential of all you could become—still, even if you feel you have failed in your Life Path up to this point. Hold up the cords you wish to break—whether these be of bigotry, selfishness or specific habits—and purify them in the radiance of the Sun of Hope. You do not need to be feeling optimistic to facilitate this—just do it anyway. Remember that each day you are reborn, and that you can show the world your new persona—you merely need to start acting it and then, be it.

As you burn away the dross of the past, note how the "lines" become golden and vibrant—regenerated by the star of their origin. See how your entire body glows with this resplendence, and be aware that this will be visible to all with inner vision, and that it will have repercussions both on how others perceive you and on your life in the most general sense.

Now you are standing upright, the dust at your feet all but dispersed, feeling positive and cleansed of all past actions. Do not, like a Catholic, feel that you are free to repeat your cycle as long as you do this visualization afterward; make a permanent commitment to change. You will be amazed at how, if you are genuine and devoted to your ideal, life flows in order to facilitate it.

Keep Khephri's regenerative light in your throat and heart, and if you feel tempted to fall again, remember it and its origin—a symbol of hope to mankind. The dark forces that propel you to weakness are those that wish to destroy life and love on our planet—while those which are preservative, like Khephri's, are here to fend off negativity and allow us to grow and reach for the light.

Strength is essential in order to attain happiness—strength in adversity and against the "temptations" of this plane. This does not mean that one should live like a monk or nun; rather, that those vices that are pernicious to us should be stemmed at the source.

Chances are, if you have performed this visualization, you have dealt with the symptom rather than the cause. This is a good start, as often symptoms can be as damaging as causes; but now, to cauterize the matter, you should bravely confront the root of your habits in order to prevent them ever recurring.

Deities such as Siva, Krishna, and Kali (for the latter, see *Invoke the Goddess*) should also help with this.

MUNDANE ARCHETYPES

The Khephri-man is self-made, an entrepreneur, and one who shines brightly when inspired. He is not ashamed of his humble origins, and may well carry the accent and habits of his roots into high circles, to prove a point, and also because it is natural to him.

Khephri enjoys every aspect of life, always finding something in it to interest him. He is a man of habit, enjoying particular rituals and their repetition, which provides a solid foundation for his high-reaching life. He is the sort to like a particular holiday resort so much that he buys a villa, and then goes there every time he needs a break. He will claim that a change is as good as a rest.

The factor defining the Khephri archetype is its constant ability to find new solutions to problems that are practical and active rather than theoretical. His failings may include resistance to ideas coming from outside his sphere, xenophobia, and the tendency to become wrapped up in his own affairs to the exclusion of a wider perspective.

TAROT CARDS
The Sun, Death, The Magician, Ten of Pentacles

RA

The golden child crawls into the Eastern horizon. A breeze carrying the scent of lotus ruffles his burnished hair. He has emerged from the center of the flower that floats on Nun, the primordial waters, and thinking of the place of safety he has left, he begins to cry. As each tear drops, it becomes a race of men. The men look up at the dazzling infant, and raise their hands to him. The boy becomes a man.

Ra strides across the sky at noon, visiting each of his twelve domains, receiving rightful worship, accompanied in his transiting by processing priests fresh from lustral baths, lotus-scented. As the uraeus between his brows spits violet fire, Ra enlightens and gives structured sounds on which to hang our human thoughts. His priests become articulate, transmitting lofty concepts that scribes record in the holy name of Ra. Pomp and ceremony accompanies the great god's every move, and he is happy.

The other side of the arc.

Ra is descending now, leaning for support on a strong stick, staggering a little with fatigue. Down below, some men still give thanks, but others, at the sight of the encroaching dark, lose faith and bewail their lot. The old sun god is dead!

Their fickle natures weigh heavily on Ra, sending him down faster. And he can hear the whispers of his fellow gods, whom he created by the very codes of his own mouth, turning the words he gave them for communication of joy against him, muttering of his decrepitude, plotting behind his stooping back. It saddens him.

Once he is out of sight, Ra straightens his back and sighs. Now he may visit the Nomes of the Dead, his nocturnal domain. At least they are still pleased to see him there.

Twelve dark provinces later, Ra re-emerges at the other side of the arc. He feels refreshed, rejuvenated, and his wrinkles have transformed to childish, chubby cheeks. He wears his crown slightly awry upon his downy head. He gurgles merrily as he remembers the pure blue flower that bore him, and then, recalling his separateness, begins to cry. From each tear springs another race of men.

They worship him. He smiles.

Ra is the original Egyptian solar deity, and author of the genesis of man and god alike. He created words, and with them, worlds.

The power of the spoken word cannot be overestimated in magick and religion. It is what differentiates us from animals, the tool of our evolution. In Hindu mythology, Brahma and Sarasvati create the world through sound and word-mongering; in Egyptian myth, Ra creates the world by naming it, just as the Christian Bible states, "In the beginning was the Word, and the Word was with God, and the Word was God." Similarly, the Christian litany, constructed almost identically to the spells of many cultures, forms a living link with God.

The word becomes a foundation for fact. Ra, as king of kings, establishes kingship on earth; the word that a man is a lord makes him so. As an ancient solar deity, Ra is greatly bound up with the royal dynasties of Egypt. The Pharaoh was purported to be physically and spiritually related to Ra. So it was said. Words create realities; words and sounds in spells make changes on every level. Like a divine trinity they construct, maintain, and destroy. Thus Ra, with his power over sound and its structure, has the abilities of several deities rolled into one.

Ra uses the power of sound to generate the other gods, the elements, and, through a combination of word craft and tears, the race of men. He is said to have been self-created, like Khephri, only springing from a more pleasant source; a perfect blue lotus flower. Lotuses are the origin of many Hindu gods, including Brahma, to whom the color blue is also sacred. This flower symbolizes the many different stages of meditative and chakric development, and the blue throat chakra relates to guidance from masters, and communication. It is the point at which the spiritual conjoins with the physical—just as its microcosmic version, the throat, unites the head (celestial, refined, seat of intelligence) with the body (dense matter, force, organs that maintain our contact with the material plane).

Being their originator, Ra ruled over the gods, but unlike the Greeks, he was not eternally young, and as he grew older and more frail, disquiet spread through the pantheon. How could anyone respect a god who drooled? At the Tribunal of Horus versus Seth, Ra as Ra-Harakhte presided over their lengthy argument (see the following chapter on Horus, page 108). During this time, his senile interjections and self-concern held up proceedings considerably, and provoked an exasperated reaction in his children. Surely it was fitting that a god or goddess took over who was more in control of their faculties? The younger and more graceful deities, Isis in particular, deemed it high time that the Old Régime make way for the new one.

This, however, would not be possible until she had learned his magickal name, the vibrational key to his essence. It was through this secret name that Ra held power over men and gods alike; Isis resolved to discover it. This tale seems incongruous with Isis in general, normally a loving deity and not prone to trickery or selfish gain, but it is said that she took some of Ra's saliva, mixed it with dirt, and created a serpent. It is culturally common for gods to create other beings from body fluids such as spittle, tears, or even, in the case of Parvati creating Ganesh, foam from her skin while bathing, and dirt. This clearly reflects the combination of water and soil from which vegetation, and thus life, emanates. If a place was sterile, it had no seed of life or "god-essence" in it; hence the personal origin of the fluids, which differentiate them from plain water.

Ra was bitten by the snake Isis had created from their combined essences. Because it was not made by Ra, and thus he could not access its essential vibration, he was powerless to counteract the venom. Dying, and in terrible pain, he cried out for help. Isis came forth, promising to heal him with her own spells if only he would tell her his name.

She had the old god over a barrel. He knew his only chance of relief was to give her the information she required, but then, he was as good as handing the worlds over to her. The agony caused by the bite, however, was Ra's immediate concern. At the end of his tether, he made Isis promise to keep his name secret from all but Horus. Isis agreed, and received the key to all creation from her anguished elder. She duly cured him, but with his recovery, he was superseded by Isis in magickal ability.

Mankind also plotted against Ra. As a sun god, benefactor but also parcher of crops, he was held in nervous respect by his worshippers. This scorching-side was seen as a punishment sent by the Ra's right-hand gods, and is personified by red-haired Set and fierce Sekhmet, the celestial lioness. She became "the Eye of Ra," in other words, the sun. The Egyptian sky is characterized by divine optics; the planets are either Thoth's eyes, Horus', or Sekhmet's. Sekhmet was the flip-side of Hathor, usually cow-heavy, protective, and ruminatory, but as a tool of

Ra's revenge on mankind, lithe, bloodthirsty, and relentless in her vengeance. (For details on Sekhmet, see *Invoke the Goddess*) So thorough was she, and so carried away by her task, that she became the Egyptian equivalent of Kali, and the world was awash with blood. Just as Siva had to pretend to be dead in order to prevent the normally mild-mannered Parvati in her Kali-aspect destroying the world, so too did Sekhmet, personification of the anger of Hathor, have to be tricked into halting. Ra mixed red ochre with fermented barley, creating a beer that looked like blood. Sekhmet drank it all up greedily. She conformed to the Dionysiac spell (see the following chapter on Dionysus, page 191) by falling asleep, and thus forgetting her anger.

One of the most characteristic traits of Ra is riding his solar barque across the sky; in other words, "navigating" the sun's diurnal course. Other gods frequently ride with him, and the righteous soul after death is carried on the barque of Ra to be placed among "the stars that never die." He is often represented as a red or orange sun aloft a boat. His other symbols include the ram, relating him to Atum, the uraeus (worn by the Pharaoh in regard to Ra), the falcon, which of course links him with Horus, one of the gods who superseded him in worship, the lion, and the ubiquitous primitive totem of virility and lifeblood, the bull.

As well as the lotus, Ra is associated with the phoenix, in the form of which he is sometimes said to have arisen from Nun, the primeval waters. The sun-bird that rises from the flames and embers seems a suitable form for a god whose name means, simply, "sun." Another version gives him, as mentioned, the form of the bull, where he appears as a calf in the morning (following a bloody looking dawn), fully grown bull at midday, when he fertilized his own mother (in other words, renewed the cycle of his origin by injecting his energy into it), and then, like all solar deities, he dies in the evening, to be resurrected the following day.

Another cow mounted by Ra is Nut, though this is said to be through fatigue rather than virility. Exhausted by his efforts, having spent himself on his creation, and saddened by men's disrespect and vice (like

God of the Old Testament), Ra is said to have rested on this goddess' back. She subsequently rose into the cerulean, her natural province, apparently with all of the other deities clinging to her simultaneously. This must be an analogy for the gap, so obvious to mortals, between the gods and humankind. They are lofty, while we are confined to earth by gravity. It is common in orthodox religions to see this as a punishment or result of the iniquity of mankind.

When Ra was missing from the sky, Thoth, the personification of the moon, replaced him. Thoth, as we have already seen, is also deeply associated with magickal arts. He signifies learning and personal effort and achievement, while Ra, however, represents the established order. Under the intuitive influence of the moon, it is possible to establish a more personal rapport with the cosmos than that which is the product of the "factual," daylight hours that are Ra's domain. Hierarchy, material wealth, and the need to strive on the material plane are most people's day-to-day experience. At night, however, recumbent and surrounded by shadows and tenuous light, we are free to envisage a more profound state of affairs, and to attempt to manipulate the substances of our existence, which are infinitely more malleable at such times. Thus it is that Isis and Thoth, both moon deities, replace the solar Ra, bound up in pomp and ceremony, in the realms of magick. A modern equivalent is the replacement of High Magick with a much freer form of mystical expression—the eclecticism and improvisation of Wicca and many other forms of Aquarian spirituality. Likewise, the protocol and ceremony of the Christian Church is finding itself outdated. Even the strictest bastions of ages-old Christian worship are finding it necessary, like Ra, to flow with the times. Inflexibility is death to any régime.

Separated from men by this distance, and physically every night when the sun has set, Ra's troubles were far from over. The terrible serpent Apep continually threatened to engulf him, and he traveled from plane to plane in the Underworld in peril, a comfort nonetheless to those who abided there. In the morning he returned, casting himself in relief into the sky and shining down on the populace below.

Ra represents the "ages of man" given to Oedipus as a riddle by the Sphinx. He is a child in the morning and thus "walks on four legs"; a man at midday, a biped; and an old man leaning on a stick, a "third leg," in the evening. He could be said to represent mortality, while later gods represent immortality. Even though Ra sets and is resurrected in the morning, it is through Osiris that the Egyptian mind finds its symbolic perpetuity. Osiris is dramatically slain by Set, but finds his redemption through love; the vivifying quality of his wife Isis. With her magickal arts, she is better equipped to aid Osiris than are Ra's habitual companions: Nut, Maat, and Hathor/Sekhmet. Because Ra has created all, there is nothing "outside" that can help him. Osiris, however, is one of several sibling gods, all very different, and it is possible to find complementary opposites within this system. Isis comes nearest to an opposite of Ra, with her lunar associations, youth, and cunning.

Because of Ra's connection with the royal family, renowned for their intermarrying—brother with sister, son with mother—very appropriate to the Oedipus myth—it is tempting to view the degeneration of Ra as an early perception of the need for "external" genes. Naturally there would have been no scientific basis for this concept, but Ra, often depicted later on as crippled and drooling, may have reflected some of the bizarre and presumably rather obvious physical results of Egyptian incest. Horus, too, is sometimes depicted as crippled or lame, though this is largely due to his enemy uncle's continual assaults on his health. Horus' parents Osiris and Isis were also brother and sister, but as sun and moon they also represent polar opposites.

For us, the main significance of Ra, however, is not his decrepitude, but rather his initial ability to create and sustain through the power of sound and word. All spiritual aspirants emulate this, whether through heartfelt prayer, chants, or spells.

Contacting Ra

The best time to access Ra is at dawn on a Sunday. Greet him with the sunrise. Burn incense such as frankincense or a solar mix, and hail Ra out loud, if you are able. Obviously it will be easier to perceive the old sun god during summer, but even if the weather is dismal, be sure to visualize him rising in golden resplendence, a bright solar disc beginning its course across the sky, or a crowned king; whatever you prefer. Envisage the brilliance behind the clouds, or, if the sky is clear, augment the natural light with your own imagination. The brighter and stronger your creative visualization, the more powerful the result.

Visualization for Effective Spoken and Written Spellcraft

This exercise does not apply merely to the student of magick. It is pertinent to any who use words for communication—and the more creative the endeavor, the better. Poems are often like spells, and a well-written novel holds its reader captivated while the scenes play themselves out before the inner eye. The writer has induced a state of creative visualization.

So, this exercise may be used to aid writing, talks, and speeches of any kind, as well as spells and magick.

Assuming that you have not already begun your endeavor, gather as many pages of blank paper as you think you will need. If the project has already been started, use the paper you have already written on. If your project is on computer disk, print out at least the first few pages for use in your ritual. Place it in the center of the room you are working in.

As you hail the dawn, and with it, Ra, perambulate the room clockwise with the incense, visualizing the brilliant solar light centering itself on the pages of your endeavor. Then sit down cross-legged before them, still visualizing the light, and meditate on "OM." Imagine this churning up the primeval waters of life and your imagination, sending new ideas and life forms to the surface.

Light begins to suffuse your mind. At first it is subtle, like dawn, but then it begins to grow in intensity. With your mind's eye, you perceive the epicenter of the radiance—a tall, slim man wearing a uraeus headdress, entirely clad in fluid, heat-and-light-emitting gold. His robes are too dazzling to look at, leaving imprints on your retinas just at the thought of them.

This stately being is processing across the sky, taking the light with him where he goes. He smells of frankincense and tradition ages old. He does not look directly at you, but walks in profile. He is majestic and aloof; not a god it would be easy to supplicate, and certainly not to stop!

However, you can use the radiance he transmits to do the trick. Reflecting on the fact that water and light makes life, you allow the power of the sun to enter the primeval waters of life/your imagination. Feel them really penetrating into the depths, possibly throwing into light relief some highly bizarre images. You may want to jot these down, and interpret them later.

Now envisage the sunlight moving over these churning waters, sanitizing them. Feel the effect of order on chaos; communication borne of primal communion, the key to evolution.

As you think this, you perceive a vast black shape in the waters, so huge that at first you think it is static, despite the water moving around it. Then you catch an eye, which seems to be looking at you. It is that of a whale. With increasing awe, you realize this water is full of them. They are what Sri Yukteswar called "the whales of big thoughts," as opposed to the "darting fishes of little thoughts." They are the whales required for creative projects, of course. If any sea creature knows how to communicate, they do. Their eerie calls are like strange spells themselves, radiating through the seas of the subconscious.

If you wish, again make notes at this point. Do not use sentences, but jot down whatever words or images arise in you mind. Try particularly to use the right word, to find that exact description you are looking for. Precision is everything in magick.

The King of the Sky continues across the empyrean. He is not going to acknowledge you, evidently—the lines on his face suggest he has greater concerns at hand—but the effects of his presence are powerful nonetheless. It is time to stock up on his arcane yet vivifying energy.

Imagine your crown chakra, the lotus of light at the very top of your skull, opening out to receive the rays of Ra. Gradually, the white petals unfurl, one by one at first, and then in a full burst of enthusiasm for the sun. The light of creation suffuses the flower, making it dazzling to your inner vision, and then slides down your spinal column, suffusing that also. Keep pumping in this energy—the source of creation—until you feel you have enough inspiration to create worlds.

When you are finished, thank Ra, and turn your attentions to the matter in hand. You should feel uninhibited by convention and confident enough to "let yourself go." Write these ideas down, and link them into poetic prose for as long as you feel inspired. You can always edit them into sense at a later date.

A word about writing and other creative endeavors—spells and visualizations can enhance, but never replace, hard work. The same may be said of magick itself. In all cases, it is necessary to practice continually, using every intuitive faculty *in conjunction with* common sense.

In magick, the art of being succinct cannot be overstated. Ambivalent words and images will create ambivalent results. The fewer the words, the greater the accuracy; in spells, at least. The realms of matter, mind, and spirit have to meet—which means an equal quota of each. The key is to strive.

Visualization for Giving an Impressive Speech

Good speeches are not necessarily as succinct as effective spells, but they are equally to the point. There is greater room for pleasurable flourishes, description, and, of course, humor, but overstatement and digressions are death to an audience's willing attention span.

The most effective speakers do not preach, but allow their audience to reach their own conclusions after a few effective promptings in the right direction. We all know the tedium engendered by an overzealous speaker, religious evangelists being the most obvious example. They usually end up causing nothing but emotional overdrive, thus casting themselves down in the eyes of the less affected. Too much conviction can often have the adverse effect of sounding blatantly untrue. An intelligent audience wants to be treated as such. It is always better to present any argument in the vein of "It is my belief that . . ." rather than to state so-called "truths." The discriminating listener will not be swayed by immodest beliefs in one's unique rectitude, and the message, however worthy, will be dismissed along with the rest of the speech.

I have spent many afternoons listening to people on soapboxes in London's Hyde Park. Speaker's Corner is supposed to be a symbol of democracy, where anyone can go and have their say on whatever subject moves them. If they are interesting or inspired enough, they will attract an audience.

Unfortunately, religion is the prime mover of the tongue it seems, and Sundays at Speaker's Corner have now deteriorated into factions of Muslim and Christian fanatics. Both attract wide audiences, but they are preaching to the converted. This is a speech at its worst; a simple ego-trip, self-glorification in the name of God. It is a type of blasphemy, especially when those of other faiths or philosophies are categorically told that they are wrong. Effective speeches never do this.

The best speakers at Hyde Park are often those who are quietly confident, and wish to be involved in thematic discussion, rather than the mindless repetition of tired statements. They concentrate on the matter in hand, but maintain an open mind. In this mortal condition, who can possibly know that he or she is totally right? The odds against it are phenomenal. Clinging to or amassing a group does not make one more likely to be right, but increases the potentially for being harmfully wrong. So, the individuality of each member of the audience, along with modesty and focus, are some of the prime points to consider.

The other speakers, who will make the listeners actually enjoy the talk, add structure and entertainment value. A clear message amusingly delivered will have a far greater impact than a fanatical diatribe.

Ra, with his ability to select (and, indeed, create) the *mot juste*, and his sense of ease with formality, is the prime godform to whom to appeal with help in such an endeavor.

First, get a parchment and quill—or pad and pen—and visualize the talk you are to give as a spell—whether its intent is to entertain (such as a wedding speech), to convince (such as presenting a plan to a potential sponsor), to educate (a lecture), or to demonstrate (an office training session, perhaps.) In all cases, you are hoping to elicit a particular response from your audience; pleasure and laughter, active understanding of your ideals, comprehension, and mental participation.

Select key words that describe your message, and write them down.

Now make a list of the main points that will create the structure of your speech or talk. As you do so, imagine them being written in golden ink on ancient parchment, sun-bright words that dazzle and enlighten.

Visualize Ra processing across the sky, at first in profile, but then, at the midday point, turning to face you. His radiant visage is almost too much to contemplate, but from the uraeus on his brow, he sends out a brilliant golden ray that penetrates the top of your head and sends shockwaves of inspiration tingling through your body.

Now write your speech in full. Feel the delight of finding the precise word containing the essence of your meaning. It might be helpful to have a thesaurus and dictionary handy at this point. Always double-check any words you are unsure of; it is best to use an old favorite than misuse a newcomer.

When the words and meanings have ceased to flourish on the page, we need to cut out the superfluous points. If your speech is supposed to be of a certain duration, now is the time to read it out loud and time yourself. If it is too long, go on to the next section. If it is too short, return to visualizing the inspiring rays of Ra until you have accrued enough material for your purpose.

For the next stage, again visualize Ra, majestically moving through the sky's epicenter. In his hand is a staff, a solidified ray of the sun. As you contemplate it, it sends a brilliant emission of red-white-hot light down into your parchment. This is a ray of discrimination that will rescue your speech from unwanted detail and allusion.

Now look at your speech, and cut out the parts that seem to be highlighted by the cauterizing light. Imagine yourself delivering a message of maximum relevance and effect, with no sidetracks.

Reread your speech in its entirety, and again vocalize and time it. If you are still unhappy with the results, repeat the process. With all of these rays from Ra, it is bound for brilliance.

Do not forget to concentrate on delivery. Intonation, elocution, and articulation are as important as a good string of words. Use the age-old trick of imagining yourself on the platform (or wherever you will be), your audience before you. If you like, you could envision yourself as Ra himself, commanding respect with his majestic presence, shedding light as he speaks.

Practice makes perfect. If you trip up, continue. Don't be too hard on yourself. And most of all, enjoy it!

MUNDANE ARCHETYPES

Ra is one of whom others say "he's had his day." In youth and manhood he attained great heights; he often peppers his conversation with reference to "the good old days." He is respected for his genius and innovation in the past, but his arrogance and sometimes incoherence do little to endear him to people in the present. He is the sort of ex-soldier who tells children in the street how lucky they are, how easy they have it, and how, when I was your age . . .

The best therapy for this intelligent but somewhat eclipsed archetype is to take a graceful step back, allowing others to acknowledge the good he has done in the past, while also getting on with their own concerns and projects. He needs to accept that youth is as valid as age, and innovation as valid as tradition. Then he may take his rightful position toward the back of the procession through life, until next time, when he will find himself once more at the front. The hierarchy that created him, after all, dictated that pecking orders should exist.

TAROT CARDS

The Sun, The Hierophant, Two of Pentacles

HORUS

The Golden Infant reposes on his mother's knee.

His potential is still a gleam in his dreaming eyes; one of these the sun, an eye of worldly ambition and royal heritage, the other a lunar reflective sphere in whose swirling phantasms he learns to shapeshift, to protect himself from all Evil, and to visit his father in the Realms of the Dead.

Only child of the Great Sorceress, Horus floats on her tides and is lulled to sleep by her waves of spoken spells and promises of futurity. Her perfumes entwine with his thoughts, festooning them with potential. Every seed-thought is brought to blossom by his mother, Mistress of Magick. She tends him and prunes the branches of his mind, keeping them just and true and bent upon the destruction of Injustice and the reestablishment of Good.

For recreational exercise, he flies high into the clear blue sky on wings of gold, his sharp eyes honing in on his future King- dom, the Kingdom for which he will fight, once his father's. From the empyrean he spies out his potential subjects; those who are true to his father, and those who are fickle, slaves to Seth. He swoops and hovers, absorbing every detail. One day he will bring subject and tyrant alike to pay.

Though I am small, I am strong; though I was borne of grief, I shall bring restorative joy; though a shadow has thwarted my light from the very first, there will come an hour at which I will shine so fully that I shall cast away all darkness with my righteous light. And those shades shall not return, for the Land of the Living is mine and I will allow no plot, no lurking envy, no bent sinister to inhabit it.

All shall be scorched to purity by my Eye of Fire, and all good souls protected by my cerulean wingspan. This is my promise and my duty and my Word.

Horus, the son of Isis and Osiris, is one of the best-known Egyptian gods. The product of the two most popular deities and final member of the Trinity could barely be otherwise. His parentage is sometimes ascribed to Geb and Nut, or he is said to be the son of Ra. There are so many versions of Horus and the falcon that came to represent him, that his popularity was again ensured. His aspect changes in accordance with each, but the Horus of which we are aware today combines the most powerful and pertinent points of each. The aspect of most interest to us here is *Harsiesis,* child avenger of the murdered Osiris.

Horus is a sky and solar deity, hawk- or falcon-headed, his eyes metaphorically the sun and moon (like those of Thoth), his color often golden. The dual properties of his eyes might be interpreted today as representing equal control of the left and right sides of the brain, and thus over all aspects of Being. He also boasts a famous other Eye, all-seeing, the *Uatchat*, representative of elevated spirituality and insight. When the sun and moon were not visible from earth, Horus was considered to be physically sightless, and thus he became god of the blind.

Horus is the product of an act of necromantic magick; Isis mediates the seed of her slain husband and in grief, conceives. Horus epitomizes all of Isis' hope for the future, the hope of the prevalence of Good in the world. Horus is part love-child, the only living remnant of Osiris, and part avenger. He is born to comfort his mother, firstly as a child, then as a bringer of Justice for his father.

Seth, of course, is fully aware of this infant and the threat he represents. Horus must be continually protected from the stinging insects and biting animals sent by his evil uncle, and even his birth is overshadowed by the knowledge of a force accumulating against him. Isis delivers Horus prematurely on the drifting isle of Chemmis, chanting and weaving spells around him all the while.

Like Krishna and Zeus, Horus is raised in rural obscurity, reliant on his mother's magick as amulet and antidote to the numerous Seth-sent insects, reptiles, and ailments that plague him. He learns the necessity of psychic self-protection at an early age. Horus' battles with his evil uncle are core to Egyptian myth as we know it; though it might be noted that many innovations were introduced by the Greek writer Plutarch, whose "Isis and Osiris" (Moralia, Volume Five) is our major written source of Osirian myth (and thus that of *Horus Heriesis*.) Plutarch would of course be familiar with some of the relevant Egyptian artwork and scripts, such as those on the temple walls at Edfu, but he has embellished the tale considerably.

Horus also fights in an older aspect—against the enemies of Osiris' predecessor, Ra. As *Horus Behdety* he fought and fended off those who were plotting against his father, Ra. In this myth he took the form of a winged sun-disc, one of his most characteristic symbols, along with the Eye of Horus. The tales of the enemies of Ra inevitably became integrated with those of the enemies of Osiris; either way, the winged disc represents protection from harm, particularly plotted harm.

For many years, *Horus Hariesis* fought against the forces of Seth, often displaying considerable tactical and martial skill. In respect of this, the Pharaoh was equated with Horus, and the royal family were believed to have descended from him. As a warrior god, Horus held great appeal to the king, especially as one who is purported to be upholding Justice by combating evil.

Combat in arms, however, was not enough to overthrow the war-hardened, more experienced Seth. Try as he might, young Horus could never keep his uncle back for long. The will of both to rule Egypt was too great for either to reach a truce. In frustration, Horus decided to call a Tribunal of the Gods. Thoth presided over the proceedings, and thus Ma'at (Justice) was guaranteed.

The decision was instant and easy. Of course Horus should become king; it was his moral and hereditary right. However, Seth would not countenance such a ruling. He had Osiris brought before a tribunal in his own right, with Ra-Harakhte, resplendent in golden sun-disc wound around by a fire-spitting uraeus, presiding over the court. Ra was often purported to be the son of Nut, like Seth himself. This relationship meant that Ra-Harakhte was a subjective judge from the start, inclined to find in favor of Seth because of this maternal bond.

The tribunal dragged on for eighty tedious years, with no decision reached. Horus was on moral high ground but was still seen as a stripling; Seth was strong and capable and the son of Nut, but even his eloquent lies under oath could not conceal his essentially unpleasant nature from the judges.

Shu and the righteous Thoth recommended that Horus' moral victory should conclude the trial. Isis sighed with relief and attempted to present her son with the Eye of Royal Power. Ra-Harakhte, however, balked at the sudden overthrow of his jurisdiction, and refused to allow the transfer of power to Horus. The courtroom groaned with boredom. Would this matter ever be concluded?

It was suggested that the advice of the oldest goddess, Neith, be sought. Again, she found in favor of Horus, and all agreed; but the jealous

Ra-Harakhte, now accustomed to being the star of this show and wishing to prolong the trial, returned the court's attentions to the familiar topic of Horus' callow youth.

Clearly the Celestial Tribunal had reached another impasse.

One of the gods, Baba, shrieked a frustrated insult at Ra-Harakhte, who was so piqued that it took Hathor's love-charms to return him to the Tribunal. Plutarch has her revealing her body to the petulant god to cheer him up, though this entertaining scene has more the ring of an author's ploy than of the divine Hathor's typical behavior about it.

Isis, meanwhile, had decided to intervene. Mistress of disguise and concealment (see *Invoke the Goddess*), she transformed her face into that of a captivating young stranger, dressed herself in a resplendent robe and a tunic that fitted her like a rind, and dabbed a little bewitching oil behind her ears. Slinking into the tribunal, she caught Seth's eye. The lusty god was over like a shot.

The beautiful stranger told him of her husband's death, and of the few sheep and cattle which were left to pass on to her son. Another man, she said, had interloped on the grieving family, threatening to remove the son's effects by force unless they were given to him. Seth, enchanted by the fragrant lady, failed to notice his own deeds in the metaphor, and exclaimed upon the injustice of stealing a child's hereditary rights. Ra-Harakhte witnessed the statement, and all the tribunal agreed with Isis that Seth had condemned himself by the word of his own mouth.

Seth, predictably, would not accept a decision reached by this trickery. He proposed a grand finale; he and Horus should fight as hippopotami, and the first to leave the water lost his claim. Horus agreed, and in they went.

Again, Isis decided to intervene on behalf of her younger, weaker son. She attempted to lance Seth with a magickal harpoon, but it missed and hit Horus instead, who cried out in pain. She withdrew it and tried again; this time hitting her intended victim, who also cried out in pain. Isis, however, is renowned for her mercy, and it racked her heart to hear her brother suffering so. She withdrew the lance.

Horus, sick to the back teeth of his mother's well-meant meddling, leaped from the water and struck off her head. This detail seems to me to be particularly Greek, more the sort of thing that would happen on Olympus than in the generally dignified Halls of the Ennead, where spiritual grace is usually the overriding factor. However, as this and the other details mentioned here have become part of the Horus ethos, they are of significance whatever their origin.

So, Plutarch writes that Horus slays his mother, for which he is horribly punished by Seth, who discovers him in hiding, tears out his eyes, and buries them. The significance of the eye in Egyptian symbolism is vast, as its sacred art amply illustrates. The Uatchat (Eye of Horus) is all-seeing, and its burial takes the light of justice out of the world. We recall that Horus' eyes represented the sun and moon, and Seth's burial of the celestial luminaries is clearly a blow to mankind and to the forces of balance. In a manner that distinctly recalls Hindu mythology, Horus' eyes then blossom into lotuses. Some sources quote his nativity as that of being lotus-born, representing purity. The lotus being a flower whose perfection is clear to all—the Devic symmetry, the fragrance, the fact that it floats upon the Waters of Life, inviolate—we may deduce that Horus himself is of a pure nature. His eyes, though buried in enmity, instantly flourish with perfection. Hathor then finds Horus, restores his sight with milk (her symbol, mother love) and they return to the tribunal for a plethora of further tricks, speeches, short-term decisions, and battles.

To whom else could the court appeal for help? They had already asked advice of all the gods, and then ignored it. It occurred to them that Osiris, the only deity so far not questioned, might settle the dispute; though clearly it would be in favor of his own son. Because Osiris of the Underworld presided over their immortal souls, his judgment could, it was conjectured, be trusted.

Horus won, in the end. He became King of the Two Lands of Egypt (Horus of the Taui), much of the former roles of Ra and Osiris being incorporated into his worship. He passed into successful manhood through a series of trials and initiations, honing his skills and learning to operate effectively without the perpetual aid of his mother. He represents the stage of the life cycle which is full of promise but needs hard work and stamina to achieve success. Even the gifts of the gods are not merely given; they must be earned. Horus is the perfect example of one who strives to succeed.

Horus' righteousness is underlined by his being wronged from the start; his very nativity is facilitated in order to bring eventual revenge on his father's murderer. His solar and sky properties enhance this image, for Horus' temperate qualities are conducive to growth, while Seth's are as harsh as the barren desert. As son of the corn god, Horus is associated with the environmental conditions required to bring about a healthy crop. His mother Isis is linked with the rising of the Nile and all fecundity, agricultural and marital. The fact that Horus is a growing boy, often depicted as a baby seated on Isis' or Hathor's knee, emphasizes his forward-forging, regenerative aspects. He is the future, a young king who will bring a fresh régime. It is clear from myths in which Ra is featured as a doddering old man that respect for the "Old Régime" had faded somewhat. So Horus symbolizes the righteous, the formative, and the striving.

Horus' four sons presided over various portions of the human body after death, underlining his preservative properties, and that his influence is not merely transitory, but eternal, like the soul itself. Horus amulets are found in sarcophagi from the Twenty-sixth Dynasty onward (when deity amulets became popular in funerary paraphernalia), Horus guarding the area just above the heart, his sons that just below. This befits Horus' solar role, which is intimately connected with the heart (and back). The deity's main functions, however, are those particular to the Land of the Living, which he has inherited from his father.

CONTACTING HORUS

Sunday is the best day of the week to contact solar deities, and if it is summer, all the better.

Frankincense is an aroma that befits the golden, ceremonial atmosphere of Horus. This will channel him at the height of his magickal ability and regal status.

If possible, take a bath with a handful of salt and a few drops of frankincense oil prior to approaching Horus. Alternately, take a shower, perhaps with a frankincense joss-stick burning in the background. Yellow or golden candles will add to the atmosphere.

As you bathe, envisage yourself becoming very pure, and glowing with golden light. Feel your inner vision becoming as sharp as that of a falcon. In your bid to see justice done, you will not miss a trick. It is important to feel alert in a Horus visualization or working, so do not linger in the bath for too long. Arise in an astral cloak of gold, and hone your mind to that of the Egyptian Prince.

VISUALIZATION FOR STRENGTH IN PERPETUAL ADVERSITY

The title of this visualization may sound a little over the top for most of us; hopefully we are not as blighted by enmity as is Horus from the moment of his conception. However, this visualization will certainly help combat any recurring problem, particularly those caused by the tyranny or jealousy of others. Just as Horus' birthright was to rule over Egypt, we too have a birthright—to rule over our own conduct and be free to be happy. Any meddlesome person or group of people may be dealt with in the Horus exercise. This applies equally to those who wish to fight or speak out for justice, but who may be afraid to do so because of the actions of others.

Take several breaths of bright yellow light, concentrating on Horus as discussed above.

Now, taking several more breaths and wrapping them around yourself, feel yourself merging with this archetype.

You may now be symbolized by a winged sun-disc or a falcon-headed youth, whichever you prefer.

The source of your trials will initially take the form of a giant scorpion. As you envisage the latter, try to invest it with all the angst caused by your reoccurring adversity. At the moment, it is lurking in the foliage, just outside your sphere.

You are in a protective bower (representative of where you feel safest), daydreaming about all the lovely things you could do or have, if only you were free to follow your path of choice. It infuriates you that your rightful domain is being denied to you by this interloper; your happiness is compromised and your quality of life ruined.

As you think this, you hear a rustle in the undergrowth, and out comes the biggest scorpion you have ever seen. It is black and swaying its tail at you, trying to hypnotize, and it emanates the gall you feel toward your adversaries. It is scuttling straight at you.

You look around for something with which to protect yourself, but nothing seems appropriate for repelling the gigantic crustacean. In panic, you begin to back off, and your foot rests on a lily pad. Water! Siphon it up in any way you see fit—use your ingenuity or simply your Will—and direct the full force of it at the angry interloper.

As you draw up the refreshing, cleansing liquid, you notice at the bottom of the lake a silver Ankh. By the gentle, protective light emanating from it you deduce that it is a talisman of Isis. The whole lake, indeed, shimmers with her magickal, healing properties.

Greatly encouraged, you direct a forceful plume of this water at the hateful scorpion.

It recoils. As the water hits the shell, it boils and evaporates instantly, causing a veil of hissing steam to rise between you.

Scrutinizing the space to which your enemy was driven, you are gratified to find only a jagged-edged black shell lying in a pool of pondwater. Just as you are beginning to feel victorious, a loud, unfriendly sibilant sound assails your ears. Behind you rears a giant cobra.

Again, you need to use your ingenuity to fight it. Rather than following these instructions, why not try to kill it yourself? Remember that it represents the enmity you have faced, and the degree to which you have allowed yourself to become affected by it.

Blast it away. If this proves difficult, use the water you employed earlier against the scorpion. This cannot fail to destroy it.

Serpent dispensed with, you are just about to sit back down to reassess your lot, when a spider of science-fiction-movie proportions approaches you with hunger in its many eyes. Each hairy leg reminds you of a situation in which you have been compromised, a confidence-draining experience. The spider wants to suck the life out of you too.

Fight it. If you can destroy it under your own steam, all the better. As you blast it with your energies (and don't forget the water: it cannot fail), envisage yourself destroying the negative aspects of your past, enabling you to build a future free of these compromises. Put all of your angst over the situation you are combating in this exercise.

Recline in the bower. You may or may not be approached by further assailants. Even though this exercise can be mentally exhausting, it is worth hanging on in there until you have freed yourself of all enemies. Each one represents, of course, a factor or response in your life standing between you and success. Your subconscious will throw the images up once you have embarked on this visualization. Destroy each as it becomes apparent to you.

When you are quite sure that all hostile thoughts and situations have been destroyed, return to your room and, if possible, have an early night.

This exercise may work the first time around, but most probably you will have to repeat it several times over. Use whatever symbols of your assailants you feel appropriate. People often remind us of animals; if the hostile party is associated in your mind with one, use that. Do not envisage yourself fighting the individual, but *the negative responses they cause in you*. Assailing a personality or individual is psychic attack, a whole different ball game and one that has terrible repercussions for the perpetrator.

Always use the symbol to represent your own responses. If these can be minimized, the "enemy" will be rendered entirely impotent.

Negative situations often recur because people easily get stuck in one mindset. However steep the opposition, creative visualization and willpower combined can help you change it.

VISUALIZATION FOR NOT BEING PUSHED AROUND— POSITIVE AGRESSION

In the event that the violence you are undergoing is physical rather than just mental, do not rely on gods and visualizations alone to extricate you. One lesson I learned in such a situation is that, however unjustified the events, the gods help those who help themselves. Physical attacks cannot be fought on the Astral Plane alone; no god will come swinging down to your defense at the last moment. Physical violence requires action on its own plane. When you are being threatened, beaten, or abused, it is time to use common sense solutions. There is no excuse for physical aggression, and if you are undergoing it, take positive action, and get help. No, it is not your own fault. No, you do not provoke it. Every civilized person has the right to live free from fear of primitive man. An exercise like this can help you avoid the psychic carnage that often accompanies a violent relationship, but preventative force (help from friends, legal action) is required to fight physical force.

If you are a victim of domestic bullying, or attacks from a partner, employer, or whatever, please, do us all a favor and tell the world. Nothing strengthens a bully more than secrecy; he or she feeds off your fear. And nothing chastises them as much as public exposure. Those who use their fists to make a point do not deserve your discretion. No matter how they justify their actions, their behavior indicates that they are out of control. People like this are contrary to evolution, and a danger to the spiritually inclined, who often reason and empathize themselves out of preventative action. Never, ever, put up with being threatened, hit, or abused. Likewise, if you are the one with violent inclinations, admit it, and change. Nothing is more spiritually debilitating than this kind of behavior.

For those whose problems are mental and psychological rather than physical, this exercise should be of use. It can also be used to dispel the emotional aftermath of physical violence; but remember, the latter needs to be dealt with on its own plane.

If self-protection is not enough, it may be time to harness some positive aggression. This should only be used when other techniques have been tried and found inadequate. This visualization is for situations that require that "fire be fought with fire."

Do this visualization standing upright.

Breathe in Horus-gold light through your nose, and exhale anxiety through your mouth, until you feel capable of taking on the persona of a warrior. Make your body as golden as that of the hawk-headed Prince of Egypt.

Now feel yourself encased in an all-protective suit of armor. It is light and flexible, but infinitely durable. No dart of spite or bullet of dark intent can penetrate it.

Once you have established your psychic armor (do not forget your head), it is time to invest it with a particularly fun quality; that of reflection. Mentally shine up your armor so that it immaculately reflects whatever is opposite it.

When these preparations are complete, select a tool or weapon which seems appropriate to you and to the situation. This could be anything from a javelin to a sword to a hammer, or a fire-spitting cobra if you wish to attune yourself even more to Egyptian symbolism.

Take your weapon, feel its weight, its strength, and the confidence with which it imbues you. Imagine it in action, rightfully fending off your aggressor, teaching him or her a lesson.

Now, visualize your enemy standing opposite you. Think of all the wrongs they have done you in the past; of the fact that, despite your attempts at attaining a peaceful solution, they have not ceased to attack you; allow righteous anger to rise up in you, strengthening your reflective, enduring armor and filling you with warlike vigor.

Your opponent looks at you, surprised to see you gradually assuming the form and stature of hawk-headed Horus, avenger of wrongs, gracious Prince of Egypt. Your opponent is annoyed to see you preparing to take what is rightfully yours, and sends out a ray of venom in whatever format is usual to them. It bounces straight off your armor and back into them with the defaulted vigor of one intent on self-immolation.

Stunned, your opponent reels back. Now is your opportunity to strike.

Take your weapon, and wield it above them while reiterating the strongly projected thought (or you could say it out loud) that you will not be pushed around. It is your birthright to go about your business in whatever way you see fit, and not to be bullied into choices that are not your own.

If your enemy sends out further poison, always bounce it off your armor and return it to the sender. That way, they expend their energy beating themselves up.

Now incinerate them while they are down. Send a searing flame of disdain from your third eye area into their prostrate body, and watch them burn.

When you are left with only ashes, raise your right arm.

At your command, a wind rises and blows through the ashes of your challenger, scatters the fine dust and blows it away into star-spangled space.

Your enemy is obliterated.

Repeat this exercise as often as required to boost you with confidence, and a sense of humor, for your next encounter with the circumstance of tribulation.

Mundane Archetypes

The Horus-character is a prodigious youth, renowned for his ability to look beyond the horizon. He will attract a cult following from an early age, friends who emulate his interests and abilities, and place themselves at his shiny-shoed feet. He is conscious and proud of his good looks and eloquence. His powers are distinctly mercurial; he is a fine communicator, organizer, and a good traveler. New people and situations inspire him, and he can hold his own before an audience.

The ultimate Horus will study mythology and the occult and attempt to communicate, both verbally and in writing, his ideas about them. His knowledge will be wide, but his interpretative skills may be limited. He is tempted to use derivative ideas for the sake of expedience.

Horus is successful young in life, and may find his later life a little dull in comparison. His vices are vanity, slyness and a cold-hearted determination to achieve his "rightful lot" in life. He is keen to punish any who stand in his way, and may well do so by underhanded means.

This youthful luminary is, however, a welcome member to any discussion or practical group, particularly of a religious, especially unorthodox, nature. His enthusiasm, relentless drive, and continual research and divination into matters mean that he is a natural leader, and that he inspires others.

Tarot cards
The Sun, The Hierophant

ANUBIS

The mourners weave along the western banks of the Nile, their tears increased by the viscous incense that pours from the hands of the jackal-headed priest at the front of the procession. Although he leads the way, by magick he also supports the mummy behind, while the wife and children wail and rend their clothes for their Osiris. A thin keen rises up from the mother of the latter, earsplitting. This is one funerary procession at which professional mourners are not required.

It is a long way to the tomb, a long way across parching sands, but with dry mouths and wet faces they repeat the incantations that assure a safe arrival. This voyage of tears is but the beginning; a thousand processes of transition must be performed before the beloved is fit to ride the Barque of Ra-Osiris to stellar immortality.

*Sister kites swoop overhead, their wingspans briefly shield-
ing the ribbon of mourning humanity from the sun. Isis never
misses a funeral; it is her will to see that none suffer as she did
in search of her Osiris. She sends sympathy to the grief-stricken
and protection to the Dead.*

*Anubis leads them to the necropolis. By hook and by crook he
cants his spells, opening the mouth of the tomb to receive its dead,
a rightful communion echoed by the opening of the mouth of
Osiris. The soul's double may partake of sacred food and drink
once the initial complex rituals are performed, but first, it is time
to say goodbye to the Outside, goodbye to the screaming, howling
mourners. Above them, Isis sheds a tear of remembrance.*

*The sarcophagus is lowered into the tomb. Anubis, who
makes all bodies whole again, touches it and is transported to
within. Here he will cast his talismans, weave his magick,
ensure a safe voyage for the stripling soul.*

*His sharp eyes stare from his natron-black face, a warning
to any who might interlope on this fresh soul's property and
rights. The soul perceives his guardian; silt-black, he names that
skin; as black as the fertile verdant Delta when the tides have
receded . . .*

*Osiris in middle, sceptre-bearing Anubis to the left, Thoth to
the right of him, Horus in the north, and Seth to the south of
him, dreaming of the river tides, and lulled by prayers and
incense, the soul reposes, inviolate.*

According to Plutarch, the jackal-headed psychopomp Anubis (An-pu),
son of Nephthys and Osiris, is borne of a trick. Nephthys, whose husband is the sterile desert-god Seth, is desperate to conceive, and dis-
guises herself as her sister Isis. The fecund Osiris makes love to her,
believing her to be his wife. Anubis is conceived, but Seth finds out and
threatens to kill the child. He has recently dispatched Osiris in pieces

into the Nile; Isis in her grief forgives Nephthys and helps her to hide Anubis in the Underworld. Nephthys in turn assists Isis in recovering the remains of her husband's body.

Originally, Anubis was the major god of the dead, but the transition of Osiris into the heart of the Underworld ousted Anubis from his primary position. As guide of the deceased, Anubis performs a similar role to that played by Hermes in Greek myth, creating the hybrid "Hermanubis" in later years. As psychopomp, the transitions between states or Underworld "chambers" are Anubis' concern, and it is stated on the dead's behalf that "the god [Anubis] transporteth me to the [relevant] chamber." Once the judgment process is complete, Anubis accompanies the deceased in the Barque of Ra, often with Isis, Thoth and Khephri, to join the righteous soul with "those who are among the stars which never rest."

Anubis is integral to the Rites of the Dead. While his animal representatives scavenge the desert lands above the tomb, flocking to wherever they sense death, Anubis abides within, presiding over the embalming, the funerary prayers and incantations, and the mummification of the "Osiris" (corpse). As the Book of the Dead puts it: "Anubis hath bestowed on thee thy winding-sheet, he hath wrought [for thee] according to his will, he hath provided thee with the ornaments of his bandages, for he is the overseer of the great god."

As supplier of unguents and preservatives, Anubis evinces an apothecarial role in this capacity. He is sometimes depicted holding serpents in his hand, which represent his immunity to their venom, and his ability to turn the sting of death to the preservative of life. It has also been conjectured that the vipers relate to the time when the Pharaoh was forced to follow in Osiris' twenty-eight-year cycle, and face death at this point in his reign. Anubis, being connected with all Rites of Death, is the obvious herald of the end of the Pharaoh's life span. Reflecting this process, twenty-eight magickal formulae are recited over the dead.

In a similar vein, Anubis also presides over lustral and purification rites. He protects the innards of the "Osiris," along with the four sons of

Horus: "He who passeth through the place of purification within the mesquet is An-pu, who is behind the chest which containeth the inward parts of Osiris" (chapter 17, p. 132).

He receives gifts for the dear departed and protects the deceased and his property from harm, "that they shall not be taken away from him by those divine beings who dwell in fetters." Importantly, Anubis receives the mummy into the tomb, and performs the Opening of the Mouth Ceremony (with the help of his earthly priest) which allows the dead to eat and drink pure essences of sacred substances. He also protectively leads the soul to the Field of Celestial Offerings, where he might feed.

Anubis is one of those who presides over the all-important weighing of the heart in the Hall of the Assessors, the Judgment Day faced by all Egyptians. Anubis balanced the beam of the scales to ensure an accurate reading. He is often depicted kneeling beneath the balance, adroitly assessing the method and result of the Weighing of the Heart. The conclusion is recorded by Thoth, and decides between a quick termination in the waiting jaws of the monster Ammut, or an eternity amongst the stars.

Anubis is often described as "upon his mountain" or "who dwelleth upon his hill"—thus emphasizing his vigilance, overview, and properties as guard dog. Many sarcophagi feature friezes of jackals, reflecting this protective role. Likewise, a couchant Anubis statue appears on many canopic chests, or is painted on the sides of the vessel.

In his part-human form, Anubis protects the process of the Passage of the Dead: "the night when Anubis lay with his hands over the things behind Osiris." The "things behind Osiris" mentioned in this excerpt of the Book of the Dead include the effects of the deceased, of course, but the action also suggests personal protection from unseen attack. Osiris himself was taken by a plot formulated "behind his back," and it is natural that his representative should be protected against similar assail.

Rather as Ganesh protects Parvati, Anubis has a special role as protector of Isis. She being his aunt and guardian, it suits his canine instincts to defend the Lady of the House. It is in respect of his genus that the city sacred to him, the Seventeenth Nome of Upper Egypt, was named by Cynopolis, City of the Dogs.

Just as Isis finds symmetry in her shadow sister, Nephthys, so Anubis has a wolven counterpart, Wapwawet. While Anubis is as black as the natron which he applies to his corpses, Wapwawet is as white as their winding sheets (also called "tresses of Nephthys"). Both gods ventured out with Osiris and Thoth on civilizing missions in the early days, and both were intimately connected with the Rites of the Dead.

Because of Anubis' connection with the desert, and because he is of the dog family, he relates to the *Gimel* (thirteenth) path in the Qabalah, leading from Tiphareth up to Kether. He also relates to the thirty-second path, connecting Malkuth to Yesod, due to his role as psychopomp. This is the route by which souls travel after death.

CONTACTING ANUBIS

Walking in a cemetery is a good preamble to encountering the jackal-headed god. Imagine him wondering around it, sensitively sniffing out the various subtle substances of the souls of the dead.

A night at the dark of the moon is best. Incense should be savory and as smoky as possible. Those with a slightly medicinal edge, such as cypress resin, are particularly appropriate. Candles of black and white will create the right ambience for encountering Anubis.

VISUALIZATION FOR GUIDANCE AND PROTECTION IN DARK TIMES

Imagine yourself in the desert. This represents the situation you are caught in, from which you are seeking extrication.

It is night, and the left eye of Horus is shut, so you have no light by which to be guided. All you are aware of is your unhappy predicament between the still-scorching sand and the big black sky, coupled with an increasing thirst.

Jackals howl nearby. Their cry makes your blood run cold. They can sense death from a league off, and you know that they scavenge in packs. The thought of encountering the sharp-toothed canines does little to inspire you with confidence.

What are you to do? You do not know where you are heading; you are dimly aware of a path that led you here, a difficult one, in which you felt you had little choice, not necessarily the one you would have chosen had you been able to do so.

You feel stuck between a rock and a hard place. If you move, you will expend energy with no sure result, probably ending up even more lost than you are already. If you stay put, the jackals and the thirst . . .

Kneel and pray to Anubis. He is a guide to travelers, an Egyptian Saint Christopher. He knows the desert better than the lines in his own palm, and will be able to lead you to water and safety. Who knows, with all his magickal prowess, perhaps he can even offer you some advice.

As you send out your prayer, you become aware of a shadow, black as basalt, looming beside you. You can just make out its outlines in the darkness; it is heavy with portent. You can sense it breathing. The shape, as still as a statue, is watching you. Yellow eyes glow above a pronounced muzzle.

As he looks at you, emanating a strange smell, slightly solvent-based and spiced, you realize that this is the great Egyptian Guide of the Dead standing before you.

Ask Anubis to protect you and show you the way to safety and refreshment. Explain your predicament in detail, if you so desire.

Anubis will take you on a journey now. As you travel, make a mental note of the symbols and situations you experience; as in all visualizations and meaningful dreams, they will prove of infinite value when interpreted.

Make sure you steer the psychopomp into landing you somewhere you like the look and feel of. You can do this by mentally projecting very strongly the things, in symbolic form, you hope for. So, if you feel your dark times are caused by lack of love, envisage a generous, nurturing environment. If lack of time is your problem, envisage yourself being led to somewhere solitary and beautiful in which you are surrounded by space.

Do not quit the visualization until you are happy with the place or "state" Anubis has left you in. When your surroundings meet with your approval, you will have to nod at the god to make him leave. He may wish to linger for a while at your side, to check that you are safe. If you wish for continued protection, do not ask him to leave. He may prefer to hang about of his own accord. Once you are ready to be left, thank the jackal-headed god of the dead for his help, and open your outer eyes.

Now write down the details you experienced on your inner journey (a Book of Shadows being an ideal place in which to record such events), and attempt to interpret them. The psychological hieroglyphs which write themselves on the walls of our minds at such times cannot be overestimated. Symbolism is the key to understanding the universe.

VISUALIZATION FOR BEING FAITHFUL/AVOIDING TEMPATATION

Temptation by its very definition means being enticed into something we would not normally do, or something that we know is not good for either us or the others concerned. It has many shapes and forms, as countless myths, parables, and cautionary tales attest, and is often accompanied by that terrifying harridan, guilt. Guilt can do just as much damage as temptation, and sometimes more. It is best to avoid both, where possible.

This exercise can be adjusted to befit any situation in which faithfulness is required, though the most obvious scenario is that of a love relationship. Monogamy can be hard work, especially as it runs contrary to nature. Unfortunately, however, it is often required of us in order to maintain a particular attachment, and if a relationship is worth having, it is worth making an effort for.

Anubis is the original guide of whom we might ask, "Lead us not into Temptation, but deliver us from Evil." He escorts the souls of the deceased to the Hall of the Assessors, avoiding all that might prove distracting or dangerous to them. He leads and he protects. He follows the network of righteousness just as his jackal cousins follow the network of their pack. There is no straying outside the established order, and the canine mind means that fidelity is natural to him. This is the trait which we are going to emulate.

You may perform this visualization in whatever position enables you most vividly to imagine the scene of temptation evaded.

Take a few deep breaths while considering the situation or person which you find so alluring. Another person, most likely, or perhaps a bar—your "vice" will inform your imagination.

Once the scene is firmly established in your mind, envisage next door to it the circumstance you wish to protect and enhance. Your partner, your home; all that is causing you to act in avoidance of the alternatives.

So, you now have the scene which threatens your faithfulness, juxtaposed by the scene of domesticity, rather like two shop fronts side-by-side on the high street.

Now visualize yourself walking down the road they are on. The first you will come to is the den of temptation, but you are supposed to be going straight home. As you draw closer and closer to the person and scene you are wishing to evade, you become increasingly agitated.

A dog is walking toward you. As he reaches you, he give you a look which betrays greater intelligence than is usual in an animal. Looking down curiously at him, you notice a silver Ankh hanging from his neck.

Take the Ankh. As you do so, it sends shockwaves of resolution into your body. This is your future you're messing with, it seems to say; act prudently, or you will repent at your leisure.

The Ankh has silver chords attached, apparently limitless in length. Using all of the determination you feel to remain faithful, take the Ankh and hurl it into the heart of the situation you wish to maintain. There it embeds itself, and all you need to do is follow the thread.

The chord is pulled tight and leads you straight past the scene of temptation. However, you can feel its potential pleasures . . . the best thing to do is not to look, not to think about it.

As you realize this, a bolt of energy passes from the Ankh, through the chord and into you. You find that you are waking in perfect profile, like a hieroglyph. Not only this, but a jackal-shaped psychic helmet has materialized on you.

With the set purpose of a 'glyph and the stalwart guidance of Anubis, it is easy to follow the silver thread without a sideways glance. Concentrate on bypassing your temptations. After all, what you really want is not to be found here.

Follow the chord of silver light anchored in your true desire. It is difficult, perhaps, to extricate yourself from your immediate desires, but remember that those at the end of the thread will be longer lasting and more relevant to you spiritually, mentally, and possibly physically too.

In your own time and with your own effort (really go through the processes inch by inch), you find yourself delivered with some relief into the heart of the second scene.

Visualizations are much easier than real life, of course. They can establish mental patterns, but it is your own determination that does the real work. Spells and visualizations are, to an extent, psychic props. If you really want to resist temptation, make sure you are always focused on what you will forsake if you do not.

Envisaging yourself as Anubis when in the situation should definitely help; and I personally enjoy the idea of being a 'glyph of concentrated Will. Egyptian art lends itself admirably to such imaginings. Every line, every shape was formatted to befit a specific purpose. All was geared toward rising, after death, into eternal life. Looked at from this perspective, temptation may be seen as an undesirable distraction from our real purpose here. Righteous Egyptians "lived by Maat"; that is, by Truth and Justice, the keys to eternal life. Emulating these traits will make infidelity to your true cause undesirable. Remember what the Egyptians always held in view—the final reckoning. This does not necessarily mean external judgment—though there is something of that in it, but the point of self-assessment, when one reviews one's life and contemplates its rights and wrongs. Painful indeed, if one has not lived with integrity! And worth bearing in mind whenever temptation is in the air.

MUNDANE ARCHETYPES

The Anubis-character is not one who sits easily with most people. He is always a step ahead of convention, and is often young, attractive, and aloof, allowing others to fall for him and then leading them on a merry dance. He allows others into his psyche from time to time, especially at night and when the mood is right, but in the morning it can be as if nothing ever happened. He often likes people until they grow to like him too, and than he loses interest. His main attraction is to a challenge; be it a person or a physical feat. Almost all Anubis-men have bungee-jumped or would like to, as they love taking themselves to the edge and challenging death. They prefer the new to the old, adrenaline to alcohol, mind-expanding drugs to tobacco. They are interested in shamanic practices, but often lack the depth to follow any given course of action. They are continually on the trail of some new scent.

Anubis-men do not take themselves (or others) too seriously, and tend to laugh a lot, quite genuinely, at people they consider pompous or neurotic. An undeveloped Anubis will stop at this point; his more aware counterpart will develop into one at home in many different environments, and able to begin to take the beliefs and thoughts of others seriously. It will probably require solitude and possibly a shock, such as a bereavement, to facilitate this.

Because the Anubis archetype is flexible and thrill-seeking, he is popular company, particularly for young and undeveloped "arty" types. Unfortunately, his pack instinct leads him to place the general opinion above his own. Even if he really likes a person, they will receive the cold shoulder from him unless they can gain approval from his pack. Unless he removes himself from the influence of his peers, he will remain perpetually immature.

Young Anubis has flashes of immortality and awareness of reincarnation which he usually refutes. He would rather be out dancing with his friends. Only being brought face-to-face with his ultimate fear—real solitude—will cure him of this.

Tarot cards

Judgement, Justice, The Magician, Death

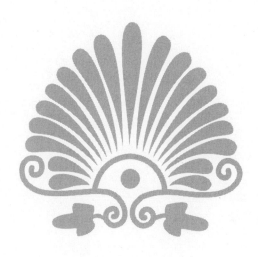

GREEK GODS

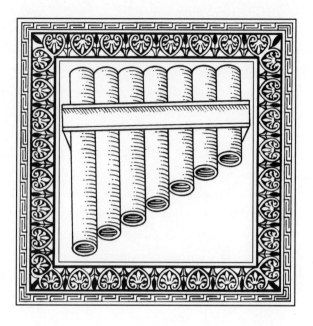

PAN

Nymphs bathe in cascading clear water.

The sweet smell of grass and pollen rides the breeze; the bleat of ewe and lamb is heard between the airs floating from the celestial syrinx. Sitting in the golden morning sun is Pan, lulling the forest with his tunes of love found and lost, rousing them with a feistier air.

Even when he dreams of the woman he desired above all others, Pan keeps half an eye on those slender nymphs. He loves to see the way the water makes a fluid cloak for their smooth and undulating bodies. He smiles as he recalls the daily chase; he hot on their tails, the sweet Nymphs fleeing, shrieking, laughing. His goat's teeth glisten through the hair around his mouth; strong and yellow, a gap between the two top front, perfect for a decent leer.

The Nymphs feel him watching as they frolic in the waterfall, and smile at him sidelong with sky-blue eyes, then turn away, giggling in clusters of playful coy. He stamps his hooves on the earth in excitement, drumming up a faster rhythm for his airs.

Dionysus comes running, flush-cheeked and glassy-eyed, his retinue of mad women and dogs not far behind, to dance a wild jig to the compelling tune. The forest is alive now; the tamarisks have exploded into blossom, ivy is twining all around them, dates have ripened in a trice and drop their succulent fruit into the festive throng. A vine has shot from seed to ripe cluster-bearing pregnancy; the women squeeze the grapes in ecstatic frenzy and, as Dionysus blesses the liquid with a yeasty smile, it instantly ferments into a drink fit for the gods that they are.

This revelry continues until noon, when Pan takes his daily siesta. He roars at them to be quiet, and Dionysus smirks at the old goat, telling him he can't keep up with the bright young things. He dances away, his ivy-festooned and shiny-eyed worshippers behind.

Pan snores, and not a bird tweets for fear of rousing him. Hands resting on his hairy potbelly, syrinx beneath his drowsing head, the great goat god dreams of the afternoon's entertainment, and of the long merriment of the night to come.

Pan has a human upper body, but the legs, ears, and horns of a goat. Sometimes he is said to be the son of Zeus and Hybris (Apollodorus); at others, of Hermes (Homer, Plato), his mother variable.

Few deities can emulate the lust for life exhibited by the god of the countryside. He is described in the Homeric Hymn as "long-haired, unkempt," joyously spending time hunting, frolicking with nymphs and "playing sweet and low on the pipes of his reed." Pan is the epitome of the free spirit running wild in Arcadia, sensual pleasure his key note as he enchants the flower-strewn forest with his music. According to this text, the gods call him Pan "because he delighted all their hearts." His roving eye and hedonistic outlook is exactly what one would expect of a fertility deity, Pan's major function.

Pan is born with "an uncouth face and full beard," causing his nurse to flee in horror. Hermes, however, is delighted by his son, fully approving of his idiosyncrasies, and to whose sense of humor a "noisy, merry-laughing child" would certainly appeal. Pan is equally welcomed by the other Olympians, especially Bacchic Dionysus. Pan becomes part of the retinue of Dionysus, and is closely bound up with this god of wine, revelry, and wildness.

In Aristophanes' *Lysistrata*, the Athenian women decide to withhold all sexual favors from their men in protest at the ongoing war with the Spartans. This creates a distinctly priapic troop of soldiers, causing the Magistrate to exclaim: "What is the reason of it all? Is it the god Pan's doing?" Clearly, in 411 B.C.E., when the play was first performed, Pan was perceived as the direct cause of male sexual excitement, particularly en masse.

However, Pan is also intelligent and caustic. In Menander's *The Dyskolos*, the god narrates the relevant details. The action is based around two young lovers and the girl's misanthropic father, and takes place next to a shrine of Pan. Because Knemon's daughter "looks after the shrine and the nymphs who share it with me," Pan decides to repay the favor: "Yes, she's so devoted and respectful to us that we've been persuaded to look after her in return." This is a role we might find more typically godlike, as is the fact that Pan is said to have taught Apollo the art of prophecy. Usually, however, we find Pan involved in more flighty activities.

Pan is the god of shepherds, and epitomizes the pastoral idyll. A possible root of his name translates as "the Feeder," relating to his position as herdsman. In Theocritus' highly bucolic works, *Thyrsis: Death of Daphnis* for example, "the horned he-goat" (Pan) is evoked amidst flowing descriptions of tumbling water, goats, kids, lambs and ewes, sloping hillocks and tamarisks, elm trees, dripping honeycombs and the ever-present music of the syrinx, the Satyr's pipes. There were many grottoes and caves in ancient Greece sacred to Pan, who made flocks fertile and spent much of his time frolicking with the Nymphs.

At noon Pan sleeps, and quietness is observed in order to avoid waking and angering him. Startled and stampeding flocks are purported to be "pan-icked" by the god, who is irascible when roused. People too are subject to sudden fear in the presence of Pan. This is partly due to the fact that he represents a complete lack of social nicety, and is powerful and unpredictable, his influence provoking deep, often unwelcome emotions; and partly because, as spirit of Arcadia, he is protective against encroaching civilization, and would scare away any who were not entirely attuned to rural life. E. M. Forster, master of the unnerving atmosphere that can lurk beneath social niceties, wrote a captivating short story on the startling effect of the spirit of Pan on a group of English tourists in Greece.

Pan is described as having "an irascible temper," and we learn from one of Theocritos' idylls that "bitter gall perches forever over his nostrils." In Lucian's "Dialogues of the Gods," Pan is spurned by Hermes for his goat looks, though other sources depict Hermes welcoming the child he sired in the form of a goat. The personal attitudes of writers always affect their art, of course, and the wry Lucian is cynical. He is pointing out the fact that most people would spurn an unattractive child. Pan, with his hairy face and blatant bad temper, is barely the typical child of a god.

Like his companions (or variable forms) Aristaeus and Priapus, Pan evinces a pronounced ithyphallic aspect. Priapus, son of Aphrodite, was sent to live in pastoral obscurity because she and the Graces found his bludgeon-like phallus distasteful. Conversely, there is no room for prissy sensibilities in the realm of Pan. Lurking in the foliage, jumping out at travelers for fun; it is understandable why such a fellow scares and causes panic.

He represents strong instinctual urges; the sort which are more often than not lurking in our subconscious. Despite his wild, uncivilized nature, Pan can help integrate the psyche and confine the wild goats of hidden desire, having let them run amuck for a while. He is, according to Aeschylus, avenger of wrongs done to animals: to which we may symbolically add the "animals" of dumb instinctual urges. No better description of Pan's power to heal (especially in a modern context) is given than in Dion Fortune's novel *The Goat-Foot God*.

Pan has appealed greatly to witches and occultists throughout the centuries, representing as he does the spirit of Nature, both in a physical sense as the untamed countryside, and psychologically, as the unfettered human spirit. The rise of Christianity and subsequent deterioration of Pan's symbology—the horns and hooves particularly—into the "Devil" icon only served to heighten the love Pan's followers felt for the great Goat God. Wonderful invocations have been written for this much-maligned Spirit of Liberty, Aleister Crowley's "Hymn to Pan" providing a striking example. In this, Crowley mentions "The tangled grove, the gnarled bole/Of the living tree that is spirit and soul/And body and brain," expressing the earth as organically and psychically linked to our spiritual progression. We, being children of the earth, are made of her matter—a fact of which Pan is the apotheosis.

For this reason, Dion Fortune saw Pan as the cosmic key to human nature. He is the liberating factor, the ability to defy the strict social order in which the characters in her novels always operate, as she did herself. Pan is lord of flesh, of animal instincts that should not always be denied, and conversely, by being unconventional, of the subconscious and its occult routes. In *The Goat-Foot God*, Hugh Paston, who is "no mystic; whatever he learned he would immediately put into practice," leans to access former incarnations by visualizing Pan in his setting in ancient Greece. It is this ability, and the "goat within" (nothing to do with sexual impropriety!) which liberates him from an impending breakdown. In a similar manner, though unspecific to Pan, do Wilfred Maxwell and Dr. Robert Malcolm of *The Sea Priestess* and *Moon Magic* respectively, break out of the their one-dimensional lives by using their subconscious to connect with the sea of occult and spiritual possibility. Pan is one of the gateways to this ocean of experience. In a modern context, this is one of the reasons for Pan's appearance on so many witch's altars.

CONTACTING PAN

The best place to contact the spirit of Pan is, of course, the countryside, and the wilder and sunnier the better. Late spring and early to mid summer are the seasons most conducive to the Pan wavelength.

Make sure you feel full of force and energy when you broach this boisterous god. He will snap a weak spine for a laugh; confidence is essential.

Music, wine, and revelry are good preambles to encountering this god. Certainly do *not* take a bath or shower beforehand; he is a sweaty and hormonal deity and you will best access him when you are too.

Ritual paraphernalia should be minimal and basic. A drum, perhaps, and a wand, the more phallic-looking the better—animal hides are appropriate, but only if the animal has been killed fair and square for food, then skinned. This is so rare nowadays that no recent hides are likely to qualify. We have no need to eat animals any longer, and the Karmic debt we owe the animal kingdom is so high already that it would be unproductive to procure a skin for this or any other exercise. In one version, Pan avenges wrongs done to animals. Best to bear that in mind when dealing with this lord of the forest.

VISUALIZATION FOR FREEDOM FROM NEUROSES AND SOCIAL MORES

If the thought of going to a party or social event makes you tense, this is the perfect visualization to help loosen you up. It is equally relevant to any sense of inhibition you wish to shed, particularly sexual. It is intended to get us in touch with the merry-making side of the psyche, the side that doesn't give a flying fruitcake what the neighbors think, or how those in our circle will perceive us. Fun is as important as discipline; both are necessary for a healthily functioning life.

You are wearing a straightjacket; the symbol of your current situation, in which you feel cloistered and unable to express your inner nature. Visualize this as a real garment. Feel how it keeps your arms rigid at your sides, and makes all of your movements jerky and unnatural.

Struggle against it for a few moments. Infuriating, isn't it?

Just as you are battling with your restrictive vestment, your ear catches a strain of music. It is possibly the most evocative you have ever heard; each note bespeaks an Arcadian idyll, each cadence brings to mind life at its most vivid and liberated. Something about it scares you— it brings to mind the expression that "the Devil has all the best tunes"— but you know in your heart-of-hearts that the source of this captivating melody is one which knows no evil, but simple pagan pleasures alone.

Concentrate on the music. Try to visualize its source; the dancing goat, legs crossed at the hoof, smiling slightly as he moves his reed pipes against his much-kissed lips. His eyes are yellow with an oval of black at the center, yet superhuman intelligence emanates from them.

You cannot fail but notice the smell of this feisty rural deity. You wonder, does he ever bathe? He reeks of the country in all its most intense forms; cow curd and goat wade fermented in the midday sun, the redolent odor of concentrated compost, almost like manure, the hops-like smell of brewing beer, and, above all, the musky scent of hormones combined with something sweaty and sharp. It stirs the blood of any who encounter it, causing animals to mate and humans to lose their heads.

The more you concentrate on the great god Pan, the looser your imprisoning garments become. Feel how, with every note you perceive floating from his pipes, a stitch unravels in your binding garments.

Carry this process through in your mind's eye, physically enacting it if possible. Bringing things through to the material realm always helps to impress them on the subconscious.

Now your straightjacket is nothing but a useless rag—cast it off.

As you do so, feel a huge influx of energy and potential entering your sphere.

You are now free to move fluidly and as you please, so if you so desire, move with buoyant steps in the direction of the enchanting music.

Pan stands at the edge of a circular bower, playing his pipes for all he is worth. Satyrs and Nymphs swirl to his music, lost in the ecstasy of movement and attunement with the Spirit of Nature. A bright-eyed Nymph runs excitedly up to you and holds out her hand.

Maintaining the thought of the music, the joyous, natural surroundings, and your newfound freedom, join in the dance if you fancy it. Practicing your lack of inhibition mentally is certainly a good way to initiate it physically.

Return to your normal state whenever you are ready. The main thing about Pan is that there are no rules except to respect the natural.

So, visit him whenever you feel inclined. Use this exercise as an entrée, but develop in whatever way you desire. You might approach Pan on a personal level, bearing in mind that his gifts can occasionally be shocking. Conventional he certainly is not, but the healing Pan offers enhances every walk of life.

VISUALIZATION FOR
SEXUAL CONFIDENCE

Be warned—Pan is not for the faint-hearted! He is the instinctual urge to procreate, a rutting beast rather than a lovemaking god. However, in this visualization we aim to temper his fertility-bringing properties and civilize them into a natural but not animalistic energy.

Pan's sexual prowess is in part due to his total lack of inhibition. He cares not a jot what the other inhabitants of the forest make of him; he is entirely happy being who and what he is. He has no inferiority complexes despite his hybrid body and nature; he has enough divinity to relax entirely into his physical body. It is ironic that this is one of the gifts that elevated consciousness can bring; a total acceptance of and exuberance in the physical condition. As a Qabalist would say, Kether is in Malkuth, or the banal is invested with God, if only we would see it.

Lack of sexual confidence is usually caused by inhibitions about the body, or hang-ups from past experiences. One of the ways to overcome it is to let instinct, Pan's quality, take over.

Lie comfortably on your back (on a bed, preferably), and close your eyes.

Imagine that you are in Arcadia, lying on the soft moss beneath a tree, your face dappled by sunlight, lulled by birdsong and the distant, haunting sound of reed pipes. The ground is cool and undulates to fit your body; you feel embraced by the earth. A gentle breeze plays over your body like the fluent breath of an Undine from the nearby brook. The spirits of Nature are all around you, and you are on their territory, but part of it just the same. They could oust you if they wished, for being from Outside, but since you are lying there so peacefully, it seems a shame to disturb you. For the sake of helping to heal humanity, they will let you stay. They hope you will not prove them misguided, however.

As you lie supine, surrounded by the exuberant spirits and creatures of Arcadia, the reality of your day-to-day life begins to slip away. It seems like so many autumn leaves, brief flourishings of circumstance, but nothing that cannot be abandoned or regrown. The essential structure of your life, with its roots in the soil, is the most important, enduring part.

Relax deeper and deeper into your Arcadian idyll. The earth beneath you reminds you that to her you will return, when your brief span in this outfit of flesh is complete. For now, it is your paradise, to enjoy and to use to the best possible end. Your body gives you an opportunity to dance to the melody of Pan, to the pure pulse of life, and to connect with the atavistic proclivities of the species. Pleasure in food, shelter, and contact with fellow humans are tantamount amongst these.

As your mind plays lazily on these topics, allow your body to lose all of its tensions and assume the ease it would have felt without the fetters of your mind and circumstances imposing on it. Imagine yourself as Arcadian; not primitive, not devoid of refinement, simply uninfected by the neuroses of your more complex life; a child born free and raised wild, like Dionysus or Pan.

As you do so, begin to concentrate green light on your entire body. Do not do this for more than one minute, but in that time, envisage your entire body absorbing and emanating emerald-green light.

The light fades, except at the base chakra, at the bottom of your spine. Visualize this growing from green to yellow, a spinning disc of vibrant light which you can feel tingling in your body; then through to orange and finally red.

Keep your base chakra spinning as you lie there beneath the tree in Arcadian bliss. Feel how it is a natural function shared, in one form or another, by all the flora, fauna, elementals, demi-urges, and gods of this rural idyll. It keeps the energy flowing, and sweeps away the negativities and considerations of the urbane on its powerful currents.

Continue this exercise for as long as you feel comfortable.

When you are ready to return to your room, visualize evening falling on the forest scene, and then night encroaching, slowly concealing the vegetation and small animals, and quieting the birds. The pipe music lingers on; there is revelry in some distant bower. However, it is not for you; your pleasure belongs mainly to this sphere.

Open your eyes, reflect awhile if you wish, and place your right hand on the crown of your head for a moment to "even out" the energies. You are now ready to approach the situation that inspired you to perform this exercise. Do so with the confidence and energy you felt during this exercise. If it begins to waver, imagine yourself lying beneath the tree again, cradled by the soft, moist earth.

Now, enjoy!

MUNDANE ARCHETYPES

The Pan archetype is found in many covens and neopagan groups, the hoary older man who tells crude jokes and slightly alarms the younger girls. In a more palatable form, he may be witnessed as the gleam in a man's eye, often accompanied by a cheeky grin.

He is natural and unpretentious and often has many animals about the house—dogs, cats, rabbits, fish, marsupials, and several children. His wife is often Wiccan and beautiful, longhaired, and big-skirted. They have a lot of laughs together, and a good social life.

The Pan-type naturally befriends Dionysus and Hermes, and the feisty band of brothers drink cider (or home-brewed wine) at one another's houses in the evenings (usually Pan's), while discussing green issues and comparative mythology (not that they would necessarily call it that); or they just chill out to music, usually acoustic and played by one or all of them. They are folky, of course, and often live in a haze of rolling tobacco smoke. They are the hub of a long-established social circle, or community even. The Pan-type attracts friends of all ages and all classes, who appreciate him for his frankness and ability to have fun.

TAROT CARDS
The Devil, The Star

APOLLO

Celestial music heralds the young god.

As he walks, flowers froth into blossom at his feet, iris and hyacinth and fragrant narcissi, and birds burst into song; almost, it seems, choreographed. He strums his lyre, music to make even the war god weep, music that heals the soul in the listening. He binds life to love with his harmonies, and season to season with his song.

Apollo's voice soothes the other gods, so often full of anger and mutual distrust, and sends messages of hope and healing to mortals far below. He translates concepts of immortal youth, immortal life, and, though they fear it is not for them, the citizens of Greece take heart at the possibility of such a fate. At least some soul is enjoying it.

Ambrosial in repose, his sharp eye chasing notes and clever harmonies, Apollo sings the fate of men and gods alike. His Priests and Priestesses bend their inner ear to the great god's song. In rapture they repeat it, the smell of hyacinths and laurel on their breath. Their supplicants thank them with honey and with gold.

Apollo is central to Greek religion, his multifaceted nature reflecting the scope of his supplicant's needs over the long duration of his worship. As son of Zeus and Leto and twin of Artemis, he is at the very heart of the Olympian family tree, his centers of worship, Delos and Delphi, as separate as his functions. Apollo is luminary, purifier and celestial musician, but he is also shooter of pestilental arrows, child murderer through pique, and lover by force. How may we reconcile the healer with the rapist, the musician with bringer of death, the precognitive faculty with the fate of, say, hapless Orestes, who was commanded by Apollo to kill his own mother? (See the chapter on Zeus for more on Orestes, page 180.)

The solar aspect is the key to Apollo's nature. In Delphi he was celebrated on the seventh day of the vernal month Bysios, as if returning from abroad—as the sun does in this season. His healing properties find an easy analogue in the transition from winter to spring, and may go some way to explaining Apollo's rhapsodic association with Kore, the youthful version of Persephone (see *Invoke the Goddess*). The subterranean maiden also returns to earth in spring, and a cross-pollination between the two is perhaps inevitable at some juncture, especially as Apollo is god of prophecy and Kore issues from Hades, the rightful domain of divination.

The strings of Apollo's lyre are said to equate with the seasons, emphasizing his pastoral role. As god of shepherds, he would again be particularly associated with spring. Apollo's amorous inclinations, which are many and varied, deepen this association. He is sexual rather than heterosexual, procreative rather than pure, full of the effervescence of spring we might associate with Pan or Dionysus. Yet Apollo is also a deity of culture, of artistic accomplishment and civic enlightenment. *Apollonian* (or *Apolline*) is the word used by Nietzsche and many after him to express structured society and its progressive qualities, as opposed to *Dionysiac* (or *Dionysian*), expressing the faculties noted in the chapter on Dionysus; those of vivacious revelry and excess. Apollo's temple at Delphi was said to be built upon a Dionysus-related enemy, the Python, perhaps indicating the transition of Apollo's function from pastoral deity to champion of the citadel.

One of the traits of this callow youth is to pursue young women, usually against their will. If Apollo began as a rural deity, his unwanted attentions towards Daphne and Castalia, to name but two, might be construed of as typical; fertility-related godforms in many cultures evince such proclivities. Even Apollo's flaying alive of the satyr Marsyas after beating him in a musical contest might be understood as the principle of survival of the fittest (or most accomplished), a function of Nature herself. The bird with the most expressive song rules the forest; communication is a form of power.

If, however, Apollo has always been perceived of as elevated in the spheres of culture and religion, his sexual behavior is deeply incongruous. No other solar deities exhibit this warp. Osiris fathered Anubis on Nephthys, true, but only when she tricked him into believing that she was his wife, Isis. Baldur of the Aesir remained a perpetual innocent, a true solar martyr. Sri Krishna may consort with numerous *Gopis,* but it is always with their consent and besides, the allegory is one of placing God-love above conventional considerations. Apollo's rape-related legends must either be imposed by human device (such as a theatrical ploy in the case of Euripides' *Ion*), or act as another allegory.

From Aeschylus we learn of Phoebus Apollo that "*Zeus endowed his prescient mind with heavenly wisdom;*" he is "*Priest, Prophet, Healer,*" and "*Knowledge of Justice and of Right*" is his. Walter Pater's *Greek Studies* summarizes the popular nineteenth-century view that "*Apollo, the 'spiritual form' of sunbeams, easily becomes . . . exclusively ethical,"* and thus *"represents . . . the sanity of soul and body . . ."* faculties barely reflected in one intent on forcing himself on an unwilling recipient. Apollo's alleged deviances are inappropriate legends for a god of purity and intellectual/spiritual elevation.

Furthermore, Apollo is said to ride sometimes in a swan-drawn carriage, a universal symbol of transcendence of the murky waters of the human condition. In Hinduism an enlightened master is known as a *Paramahansa*, a swan whose divine grace allows him to glide upon the river of life without staining his integrity. Apollo's vehicle suggests the same ability—so wherefore the accusations of rape? Certainly no Hindu god or master would be accountable for such an act. In most mythologies, it is the demons that commit the sins. We are faced with the fact that either those who participated in the genesis of Apollo's legends did not believe such actions to be wrong, as indeed a cursory study of Greek ethics indicates; or that the events described were intended, along with similar scenarios enacted by such other gods as Zeus and Pluto, to be taken as allegories. If such is the case, they may be interpreted as unsought infusions of elevated thought; sudden inspirations that leave the recipient bemused as to how to cope with the "issue." Mystics of many religions undergo experiences of divine communication, only to find themselves "abandoned" when the effect wears off and they are left with the harsh realities of the solid world. Genius undergoes a similar fate, being incompatible with mundane reality. It would be possible to attribute the shame and bitterness of mythical Grecian women abandoned by the gods to the effects of mystical aftermath—the "Why hast thou forsaken me?" principle. Just as the oracular Delphic Pythia might find her mouth "torn" by Apollo, so might a divine infusion "tear" the perceptions of the devotee. Divinity is too vast for the common experience.

We find this fact reflected in all cultures, but in Greek myth it is perhaps most obviously represented when Semele is tempted by Hera to persuade Zeus to appear before her in his full glory. (See the chapter on

Dionysus, page 191.) The result is that Semele dies, overloaded with celestial perception. So too do other characters "die," and if Apollo is involved, we might be assured that they die of shame, one of his major activating emotions. Creusa in the marginal Euripidean myth is accosted by Apollo while in a rural setting; near the caves of Pan. She is "infused"; the socially shameful issue, Ion, ends up living in a temple dedicated to his father. It would be possible to construct an argument in which Apollo is divinity unveiled, Creusa its hapless but temporarily active recipient, and Ion the exiled aspect of Creusa, which affirms the validity of the experience. Parallels might be drawn with those who have undergone mystical (particularly solar) experiences; but would this be an appropriate and true analogy for the experience of Apollo?

As god of initiation, we may again equate unpleasant but formative experience with Apollo. Apollo presides over young men as they pass from boyhood to manhood, just as Artemis guides young girls toward womanhood. In a similar manner to Persephone, Apollo's initiate might be plunged into the Underworld of his darkest concerns—though obviously the average Grecian mind would not have construed it as such—and be forced to sink or swim. In the case of Castalia, who dives into a well to avoid Apollo's advances, the result is a watery grave. Perhaps she preferred aquatic calm to the acute illuminations proffered by Apollo. (A Qabalist would say that she had fallen on her own sword between Tiphareth, to which Apollo is attributed, and Binah, sephirah of synthesis and abode of the Cosmic Well.) Orpheus, Apollo's son by Calliope, descends in a most pronounced manner into the Underworld in search of his heart's desire, Eurydice; his music, a gift of Apollo, is a weapon to him in the chthonic gloom. Orpheus physically enacts the subterranean, initiatory aspect of Apollo. In some respects Orpheus represents the sublimity of the Apollo principal, while Apollo depicts its fallible genesis.

Either way, Apollo spurs his loved ones towards a higher state of understanding by challenging social mores and more importantly, the Fates themselves (as represented by Orpheus' quest to retrieve Eurydice, or

Apollo's interference with "Destiny's primeval claims" in the case of Orestes). It is simply ironic that Apollo is one of those suspected of implementing standards and laws in the first place.

Another Apolline parallel with Asiatic myth is the principle of Karma. In Greek mythology Apollo is one of those who inflicts Karma on mortals; the disease and pestilence shot from his bow punish those who have offended the gods, either by omission (of due sacrifice), or by hubris (such as Niobe, whose boasts of fertility terminate her own issue), or by tampering with the interests of one of their favorites. In Hindu belief disease and misfortune also follow wrong action, but personal integrity is paramount, as opposed to the arbitrary whims of the gods. Still, Karma it is, and Apollo is one of those who pursues mortals to the ultimate end of their (or their family's) fates. His oracle orders Orestes into matricide, and like Artemis he will tolerate no insult to his family or to the principles he holds dear. He punishes Midas for greed by giving him the ears of an ass, and is himself punished by Zeus for killing the Cyclopes. The Scales of Justice are permanently twitching in Olympia, but are they weighted fairly?

Through the accounts of a plethora of authors we witness a god who is passionate, vengeful, fallible, and has exacting standards but fails to live up to them. Apollo, taken in his recorded entirety, is all too human. While keeping an open mind, I believe we need to discriminate as to our sources. If we are indeed looking at a god, rather than a hero, the divine aspects will be pronounced and the faults subdued. After all, apart from the odd supernatural power, which any mystic can master, what else is there to differentiate Apollo as he stands from an ordinary mortal? Where is the godlike grace, the spiritual integrity, the compassion? If Apollo is indeed a god, his myths have become obfuscated by storytelling. If his story stands as is, inclusive of the many literary tributaries, he is merely a brilliant character in an epic of human error.

Above the temple at Delphi was written, "*meden agan*," or "nothing in excess." The path of temperance equates better with the idea of Apollo as divine, and clashes with some of his steamier myths. Indeed, it clashes with most of them. In virtually every instance Apollo is impassioned for one reason or another. Sometimes it is difficult to understand why he is popularly vaunted as a deity of logic and thus, of considered action.

Nowadays, this paradox works. Western society is gradually allowing itself to be human and also to ascend; we are accepting our faults, learning from them, not permitting them to hinder us on our quest for union with godhead. However, in more stringent times the Apolline contradictions would have been an anomaly. And even in this day and age, we expect a more wholesome example to follow.

In part Apollo is traditional, a defendant of established paths, and in this capacity are his "faults" apparent. Alternately, he is innovator, bringer of sanitizing order.

Despite the fact that Apollo is supposed to represent intellect, his half-brother Hermes easily outwits him on a number of occasions, not least when he steals Apollo's cattle and extricates himself by means of the lyre, which he chances to invent. Hermes exceeds Apollo in *nous* and invention; besides him Apollo seems guileless and rather stupid. How is it that a god of enlightenment may be overshadowed by a god of thieves? Easy. It happens every day in the "real world." Hermes exhibits the sly traits of which Apollo, straightforward and solar as he is, is entirely innocent. Hermes is master of luck and windfalls; Apollo on the other hand gains and gives his boons in a structured and predictable manner. In a similar pattern will the sly always outwit the upright; because the latter do not suspect, and are too self-correcting to find as much fault in others as they find in themselves. Also, it is possible that Apollo takes himself too seriously, as do many solar deities. Those associated with Tiphareth are prone to forget that God likes a laugh, and that no amount of philosophizing or pursuing justice can compensate for the lack of a sense of humor. Hermes, of course, is one of the Olympian clowns, and it is perhaps because of this that he gets the better of Apollo on occasion.

Apollo's solemnity is most in evidence when he is scorned. It runs in the family. Artemis defends her brother's pride by killing Coronis, mother of Asclepius by Apollo, for infidelity (some say that Apollo did this himself), and the huntress is renowned for the ferocity of her responses to disrespect. In *The Iliad* Apollo avenges an insult to his priest Chryses by raining deadly arrows on the Greek army. Likewise, when Niobe slights the procreative powers of the twins' mother Leto, and stops the Theban women from worshipping her, Apollo and Artemis strike down each and every one of her twelve children, causing petrifaction to seem a better option to Niobe than life itself. A grueling description of this may be found in Ovid, and though one is riled by Niobe's arrogance, by the time only the youngest girl remains, the reader cannot help but wish for her reprieve. However, Niobe is perpetually boastful, and one daughter may produce ten grandchildren, which chaste Artemis and effete Apollo could never countenance. To make quite sure, they kill her too. Now, nobody can contest the position of their own mother, Leto. Pride and vengeance play a primary role in Apollo's character.

However, this cannot merely be attributed to the superficiality of the Grecian pantheon. As a godform Apollo is far from alone in such proclivities. The gods of most religions are fierce and merciless when crossed; the Old Testament is full of threats and punishments, as is the Rig-Veda, in which presumption is cauterized and humility rewarded. The same might be said of the Aesir and Celtic and Slavonic deities. Only the Egyptians seem to confine their judgments and punishments to other immortals; they also fail to interact with humans on a petty level as do so many other pantheons. The Pharaoh and sacred servitors are in their special care, but no affairs or vengeances are indulged in. Judgment comes in the Hall of the Assessors, after death. Apollo and his kind effect theirs in a trice; Karma is instant when the Scales of Justice are in their hands. It seems that it is Apollo's solar-logos radiance and later associations alone that justify his reputation as champion of "sanity of soul and body."

Apollo has no childhood, but evolves from babe to young man after a few sips of ambrosia. As a symbol of initiation into adulthood, his first act is to slay the Python of Parnassus, a Hera-sent threat to his mother Leto. On the spot of his victory Apollo established his sanctuary; then he endeavored to expiate himself of the murder. Not until he was cleansed could Apollo truly be crowned. He proceeded to hijack a Cretan ship and force its sailors to become his priests, barely the act of a deity whom we might find loveable! However, it's all in a greater cause. This became the site of his oracle at Delphi, even today recognized as one of the most significant spots on the geo-cosmological map.

Of solar and evolutionary gods Apollo is the only one to escape sacrifice. Ra is tricked and superseded by Isis, Prometheus pays nightly for his gift of fire to mankind, Osiris is slain by Seth, scattered, and eventually resurrected (at least, in part), Arjuna as chela of Krishna is forced to slay his own kind, Odin hangs for nine days and nine nights on the Yggdrasil Tree, sun-bright Baldur is laid low by a mistletoe arrow of spite, and Jesus Christ, the most popular solar prophet in the West, suffers, "sets," and rises again. The closest we get is Apollo's servitude to Kings Laomedon and Admetus, each duration as punishment for crimes against Zeus. The chores are chastening, perhaps, but barely the martyrdoms undergone by others represented by the same life-giving star.

Apollo's attributes of music and healing are perhaps epitomized by his own issue—Orpheus, and particularly Asclepius. In Orpheus we find a deity of impeccable integrity, one who loves with purity and abundance, the beauty of whose music echoes his inner harmony. He captivates even grim Hades with his melodies, and like Apollo, entrances animals and humans alike with his lyre. In some respects it seems as if Apollo's sublime qualities have been absorbed by Orpheus, who exhibits none of the faults of his father.

Asclepius as healer and god of medicine sent prescriptions to his supplicants on the wings of sleep, just as Durga sends healing via soma and Isis through symbolic dreams. It befits the Olympian pecking order that physical ailments are Asclepius' domain and spiritual healing and cleansing Apollo's, but on what grounds does this god elevate, purify, enlighten? One might think that there is little in his legends to justify a position of spiritual or even intellectual eminence. However, the ancient Greeks had standards so far removed from our own that Apollo was sublime simply by birthright, and is free to act as he will without threatening his essential divinity. Thus, he may indeed elevate, purify, and enlighten, as he wishes.

How to get to the true spiritual source of Apollo?

Looked at in Qabalistic terms, Apollo's contradictions present far less of a problem. As a solar deity, a demi-urge resident in Tiphareth (see Glossary, page 213), he reflects the Creative Integrity, hence his brilliance, but he is a projection several Sephiroth below the ultimate, Kether, which in itself is not God, but merely the closest proximity to God; thus there is plenty of scope for fallibility. The vice of Tiphareth is Pride, one of Apollo's most poignant traits. Its special property is Healing, one of Apollo's major functions. It evinces a pastoral theme, being the abode of many fishers and shepherds of men; we have already noted the rural role of Apollo Nomius. The particular property of Tiphareth is Beauty; one characteristic of Apollo which is never in doubt (although his allure is another matter).

The God-aspect of Tiphareth is Eloah Va Daath, meaning "Son of Knowledge," and although Zeus might admittedly be ill-appropriated to represent this particular virtue, he is renowned for his forethought (in *The Odyssey*, for example, Odysseus is referred to as "*Peer of Zeus in forethought*," explaining his navigational skills—on the waters of Life) a quality pertinent to Tiphareth whose full glory must be concealed from man for fear of overloading our senses like Semele's. Tiphareth translates divinity into a form comprehensible to us, just as Apollo suggests solar resplendence but exhibits faults enough to temper our awe. The mundane chakra of Tiphareth is the sun, the physical representation of Eloah Va Daath in the Universe, and we look at or fly close to this at our peril.

Tiphareth is the sephirah of mystical infusions, taking us back to the argument in favor of rape in Greek mythology as an allegory of shattering downpours of divine energy. In Jewish lore Tiphareth represents God as Messiah and consort, divine husband, while Malkuth is the Shekhinah or Bride of God. Energy is believed to descend the Tree at various significant times, not least every Friday night at midnight, when amorous energy from Tiphareth is received by Malkuth. Yesod helps to diffuse this; without the solar power being "eclipsed" by the lunar sphere, it would blow the lower levels apart. Again, we find a parallel with Apollo and Zeus' downpourings of affection into human vessels all too often broken by their sacred force.

Placed upon the Qabalistic Tree of Life, Apollo's cosmic role makes a holistic sense that it does not when perceived as a solitary golden thread in the Olympian tapestry. From Tiphareth we attain a clearer view of the overall pattern, and Apollo, witnessed as a solar highlight in the universal cloth, regains both his integrity and his divinity.

Having reassured ourselves of Apollo's integrity—not necessarily by the process described, but perhaps through meditation on the supple golden god, or through reflection on his myths and what they tell us of Apollo and the society that bred him—we are free to interact with him in a potentially positive sense. However, with all Greek deities, particularly the males, it is important to be aware of their dualistic natures. They are not primarily concerned with humanity's needs, as are most deities: indeed, in *The Iliad* Apollo makes the celestial apartheid clear: "Never shall they (god and mortal) be like each other—the tribe of immortal gods and the tribe of men that walk upon the earth"; and they do not seek to transcend their own vices, a distinctly Judeo-Christian concept. It is their humanlike nature that has created one of the most distinctive and popular pantheons. The Greek gods lend themselves perfectly to literature and art, as the numerous texts and statues still extant bear witness. It is thanks to their flexibility and distinctive temperament that we are able to access them today through a wealth of ancient creativity. We must also bear in mind that the authors are necessarily subjective; Homer's pantheon, for example, is quite different to that of Empedocles and Plato.

Apollo, incidentally, was said to be the father of the latter, underlining his importance in philosophical and intellectual pursuits.

CONTACTING APOLLO

If you have managed to wade through the essay above, you are halfway there already. In his intellectual aspect, Apollo does not come cheap. He requires effort, and rewards this with enlightenment. He is the god of communication of abstract ideas. The best preparation for contacting him, at least in his most advanced form, is to do some deep intellectual work, preferably including both acquiring and interpreting knowledge. Studying the wealth of literature available on Apollo is a perfect example.

The number seven is particular to Apollo, so working on the seventh day of the week—Sunday—befits both this and his solar correspondence. Most important though is the element of inspiration, which Apollo, friend of the lovely Muses, will best respond to. So make sure that you strike while infused with passion rather just because it is the seventh day, or whatever. You can always light seven candles—preferably of yellow or gold, symbolizing your awareness of the number best loved by Apollo.

A bath with salt in it is definitely a good idea prior to visualizing Apollo. Raise the salt into the ether before putting it into the water, and visualize it glowing with white-yellow light. When in the water, see your aura and chakras becoming clean and radiant. (For more information on chakras, see *Invoke the Goddess*).

When you leave the bath, make sure (by checking with your mind's eye) that you are fully cleansed. Apollo does not appreciate psychic miasma.

Incense always helps to create an appropriate ambience and, most importantly for Apollo, to cleanse the bodies. Frankincense is a good one for this solar deity. If you wish to be really authentic, add to the disc a dried laurel leaf. This was the smoke in which his Pythias sat when delivering their oracles.

VISUALIZATION FOR PRECISION WORK

This visualization may be used for everything from healing, to intellectual acuity, to mentally prising out a problem that is polluting your life. Having studied Apollo's many aspects, you will be able to work out for yourself appropriate ways to develop and use his energies. Figuring such things out personally will greatly augment their power.

Apolline intent is as sharp and to-the-point as an arrow shot by the immaculate archer. You need to home in on exactly what it is you intend to do before you begin. Woolly thoughts will bring uncertain results. Imagine your aim very clearly.

Now take several breaths of glowing yellow light, filling your lungs and body with the living power of the sun. See the room around you being illuminated by this supernatural, yet ultranatural light.

Imagine the goal previously decided as a cluster of fast-moving golden energy in the air just above you. Determine to launch it into the realms of the Actual.

Visualize Apollo standing before you. He is immensely tall and strong, like a giant, but there is nothing coarse about his smooth-skinned, fluent-limbed body. He emanates light of almost pure gold, and his hair is made up of patterns of incredible intricacy. He is smiling quietly to himself, one hand resting on his bag of arrows. In the other he holds his golden bow.

As you visualize the awesome god, you begin to hear music. Faint at first, delicate as lace or gold brocade, ineffably beautiful. This must be what people refer to as the Music of the Spheres, or a Chorus of Angels. As Apollo grows in intensity—you begin to wonder when he will stop augmenting this radiance (how much more can you take?)—the music too increases in volume, weaving its blissful interlacing harmonies around you, healing and reformatting and "organizing" you into optimum shape as it goes. You feel the design of the melody; to elicit the best from the best. It is a distiller of the soul, a catalyst of excellence. Only that which is pure and perfect is of interest to Apollo.

Allow this music to delight your inner ear and hone your sensibilities to the matter in hand. Allow what is superfluous to float away on the drifts of passing music. You should be left with shining ingots of perfected intent.

When you are ready, ask Apollo to shoot your intent into the material realms for you. If your aim is healing, ask for it to be shot at the person concerned. Never attempt to do anything harmful with these exercises. You will find yourself cruelly punished if you do.

If your aim is mental ability, ask for it to be shot into your mind, activating the desired result. If it is for purification, again, ask for the arrow to land at the specific target you are indicating to Apollo.

If he agrees, Apollo will then take an arrow from his bag. As he does so, see the golden energy of your aspirations being sucked into the arrow's point. Invest it with everything you have concentrated on previously, as well as your heartfelt desire and belief.

Apollo draws the bow and aims your arrow. You can see him concentrating on your mutual goal, his perfect vision cutting cleanly through every obstacle as if it were mere air. His taut muscles bulge with the concentrated tension of drawing the mighty, golden instrument. A moment of suspense, and then . . .

He shoots.

Watch as the arrow lands at the very center of its goal—you, perhaps, or a person or situation absent previously, but now clearly visible to your mind's eye.

The archer stands back in the afterglow, a slightly smug smile hovering on his lips. It was too easy, really! Child's play! No, no, please don't thank him. Oh, all right then, just a few words of adoration will do . . .

Thank Apollo for his help, and wait for him to leave you.

You may now go about preparing for the mental and physical manifestation of your aspirations, which are as sure, thanks to Apollo's help, as tomorrow's dawn.

Visualization for Athleticism

Apollo is intellectual and mentally fleet, but his strength and sporting prowess are equally undeniable. Physically, Apollo is a force to be reckoned with; fluent of movement, precise of aim, and full of youthful vigor. He is therefore an ideal godform to emulate in the cause of sporting ability and all-round fitness.

The keynote to Apollo's skill is the artistry with which he operates. Nothing is brut, all is refined and honed to optimum aesthetic as well as practical effect. Like Artemis, he uses his sharp intelligence to engineer his body into optimum performance. Gay men have the corner on this kind of perfected masculinity, as a cursory glance around any gay bar will indicate. Its occupants exhibit, more often than not, a classical Apolline physique unrivalled by the heterosexual community. The cult of masculinity has here been brought to a crescendo, the fact that it is for the pleasure of men underlining its polarity. Contrary to popular belief, there is no creature on earth as truly masculine as a gay man.

It is possible to emulate Apollo both for his technique and the body thus created.

Apollo is rooted in logic, so the first step is to formulate a *training plan*. Discipline is important, but so is pleasure. Apollo disdains all that is not of his own volition, and in training it is important to maintain balance. Pushing yourself too far too fast will simply cause injury. Regular exercise of a demanding but not overwhelming nature is required.

Next, we need *commitment*. This is echoed in the regular nature of the exercise and visualization. Daily is best.

Because of his solar nature, the most advantageous time to access Apollo is shortly after dawn, so the ideal time to embark upon this exercise is first thing in the morning.

Finally, *self-belief*, and the ability to visualize yourself succeeding at your endeavors, will help solidify your efforts on a physical level.

For this exercise you will need a small pot of massage oil, olive oil, or cream if you prefer. Olive oil is a good traditional substance with the right correspondences for this exercise. It was used to revive Odysseus' body when he was washed ashore following a shipwreck, and is a wonderfully solar unguent.

This is an idea for visualization combined with physical exercise. It can be adjusted to suit any regime, and may be repeated as often as required.

It is preferable to work outside, in the first light of day. If you are inside, make sure you are standing in natural light.

Hold your pot of oil or cream toward the rising sun. Envisage an arrow of golden light flying forth and dissolving in the substance you have chosen. If you like, you may ask Apollo to bless it. Put it to one side for use in a moment.

Shut your eyes, face the direction of the sun, and feel the Apolline light beginning to penetrate your forehead. As the dawn comes up and light begins to increase, imagine your own body increasingly emanating light. Every action you perform and move you make will double the amount of light you emanate until, at the end of the exercise, you will be as dazzling as Apollo himself.

Remember the traits of the youthful god—his beauty, strength, stamina, and intelligence, and feel these qualities being absorbed into your body.

Allow the light to filter right down to your toes. Visualize it flowing into every fiber and cell of your body. When you feel that it has reached every part of you, you may open your eyes.

Starting with your feet, envisage them golden and swift, shod in Grecian sandals if you wish, and rotate each in turn, clockwise, while thinking of how they will carry you to glory. Through the finishing ribbon, over the vaulting pole, or whatever your particular aspiration might be.

Now concentrate the light in your calves. Dip your fingers into the oil or cream, and begin to massage the muscles of your lower legs, visualizing the golden light penetrating right through to the bone, investing your body with vigor.

Next, concentrate on your knees, pouring lots of Apolline light into the joints which are so important to your physical performance. Invest them, along with the golden light and the oil or cream on your gently rotating fingertips, with the qualities of strength and flexibility.

Progress to your upper legs. Feel how they obey the command of your upper body, feel how they are amply blessed to do so. As you massage them with a little of the oil or cream, front and back, feel how wonderful it is to have a body you are able to direct with your mind; a body capable of following your pristine Will.

When you reach your waist, concentrate a particularly vivid shaft of light into your torso, and be aware of its tactility, lightness, and carefully honed, utilitarian muscle-power. Be aware also of your spine, which carries your commands and unites body and impulse. Massage a little of the substance into the firm muscle of your stomach area, again, visualizing the health and strength-giving golden light being absorbed right into your body.

The chest area should be similarly treated. Do not forget to allow the light to infiltrate to your back, too. If you can get a friend or partner to rub your back with the cream or oil while you visualize it becoming as golden as Apollo, all the better. If not, just envisage it minus the physical prop.

Then, the left arm. See it glowing fantastically with gold, incandescent with strength and ability. See yourself performing the sporting feats relevant to this limb.

Repeat with the right arm. You could, if you wish to envisage yourself fully as Apollo, see yourself drawing back the bow held in one hand with the arrow held in the other. When you shoot, make sure the arrow lands in the bull's-eye of your desire. Hone your thoughts to the same acuity as Apollo's shafts of piercing light.

Finally, lightly rub your shoulders and neck with the oil until they too are resplendent. Your head is already bathed in ever-increasing light, and by now you should look, in your mind's eye, like a sun god yourself.

This exercise should take no longer than ten minutes. It is a wonderful way to start a day, particularly as a preamble to training.

Now that your body is supple and your willpower concentrated, you are ready to dazzle the world with your ever-augmenting prowess. And as each new dawn breaks, so too will you increase in skill and strength.

Mundane Archetypes

The Apollo archetype is a luminary and expert communicator of abstract ideas. He is complex and intellectual, a master of cross-reference and footnote. He is often defined in early youth by his prodigious academic achievements, the most likely areas of interest being classics and the arts, particularly music. Even if his studies of the latter show little promise, he will be emotionally moved by music above all other mediums. He may evince an early love of opera and other classical forms in which love is expressed, especially if the latter is doomed.

Despite his interest in love on a cerebral level, he will be callow and inexperienced in it on the mundane plane. He suffers from his high-flying ideals being incompatible with the "real world." The Apollo archetype feels acutely, and loathes a *faux pas* almost as much as he detests crudity. He can sometimes suffer from shoving his "baser" feelings under the carpet so much that they later manifest as agonizing neuroses.

The Apollo man is always clean and tries to be well presented in a conventional manner. He is patriarchal and traditional in outlook, though capable of ingenuity. He is not stuck in the mud; he simply accepts the established order, and his rightful place in it.

He is always effete rather than manly, intellectual rather than physical. His downfalls are arrogance, snobbery, and spite. His therapies are friends, art, and music.

TAROT CARD
The Sun

HERMES

Giant-slaying Hermes knows no fear.

Life is a joke to him; immortal, divine, why should he worry? He will do good if it suits his mood—deliver messages, escort mortals to the underworld or through lateral transitions—it can be fun to be of use.

Then again, he might prefer to scheme a cunning ruse; select a trick from his secret box, inflict it on an arrogant sibling or puffed-up mortal. He laughs himself to sleep most nights; the puzzled face is a sweet nocturnal draught to his active mind, and puts it to rest. He is the most intelligent, the master of all, and could probably steal the very crown from his father's head, if he so wished; but he is happy as a humble son.

Equally at home in city and country, Hermes receives due worship by the connecting routes; roadside shrines at which requests and praises gather, liminal places which are neither here nor there. He casts his protective cloak over the weary and confused traveler, guiding him to his goal and blessing him with Muse-given eloquence. The traveler, when he arrives, has many a startling tale to tell, and his audience is riveted.

Hermes is the sharp-witted trickster, thief, odd-job man, and Magician of Olympus. He is usually said to be born of Maia, "the rich-tressed nymph," later part of the Pleiades constellation. As son of Zeus, he takes his rightful place at the family banqueting table, but unlike many of his siblings, he is not too proud to pour the wine or carve the meat. He is famed as the messenger of the gods (referred to in *The Iliad* as the "pure Deliverer"), and in his capacity of Psychopomp he guides the souls of the dead through the halls of Hades. One of these is Persephone, for whom he has also helped negotiate an annual release from the Underworld. Another is Eurydice, who is led, sadly, in the opposite direction following Orpheus' backward glance.

The roadside shrines of Hermes were composed of a pillar, sometimes topped by a head and featuring a phallus halfway down, at the base of which small stones were placed individually by devotees. As I mention in my book *Magic of Qabalah*, these would have been wonderful for divination purposes, particularly when stolen, or attained through a trick. Hermes' name translates along the lines of "he of the stone heap," and, coupled with the phallic pillar, indicates a much older deity than the Homeric Hermes to whom we are accustomed. There is also a possible etymological connection with the verb "to protect."

Like Hecate of the roadside, Hermes evinces a protective role towards travelers, thieves, and beggars. In *The Iliad* he is referred to as "the bright pathfinder," underlining his role as a Grecian Anubis or Saint Christopher. The guardianship of travelers makes him god of commerce. This is particularly relevant when we consider his mythical ability to get anything he wants, such as Apollo's heifers, and to strike a deal in his own favor (such as being forgiven his heist by charming Apollo with the lyre). Again like Hecate, Hermes works mostly under cover of the night.

Hermes' cunning is equaled only by his inventiveness. Because of his many persuasive charms, Hermes also became god of eloquence, which naturally relates also to his role of messenger. In Hesiod's *Theogony* we find him referred to as "the herald of the deathless gods," emphasizing his importance as announcer of what is to come, intermediary and translator from one state to another.

Hermes' innovative qualities are apparent on the day of his birth. He manages to sneak from his cradle, and immediately puts into operation an ingenious scheme for both stealing Apollo's bovine charges and flattering the gods. This involves making the cattle walk backward, indicating his control of domestic animals and animal husbandry; disguising his own tracks (by wearing self-crafted sandals), and cleverly making a fire and roasting two of the heifers in honor of the twelve gods. He offers the fruit of his cunning back to his father, brothers, and sisters, symbolic of his future use to them, and ensuring that they see the funny side of Apollo's shame. Hermes is the archetypal charmer, with whom none can remain angry for long. Even Hera likes him, bestowing on him an affection unrivalled by her other stepchildren.

Significantly, once he has stolen and killed two of the cattle, Hermes refuses to partake of the sacrificial meat himself, though "the sweet savor wearied him." The trick becomes a feat of endurance, an initiation into the art of self-control. He also wishes to make a point. As he tells his mother, "If my father will not give me [the rite that Apollo has], I will seek—and I am able—to become a prince of robbers." The phrase "I am able" is a key motto for Hermes.

Hermes is looking for acceptance in the pecking order of Olympus, and is determined to receive it, even if it means plundering Apollo's "great house" (his temple at Delphi), or, as in this case, denuding the sacred meadows of their "wide-browed grazers." As a token of this abstinence, and as a signal of the new order of things now that Hermes is born, he hides the fat and flesh in the barn, "placing them high up to be a token of his youthful theft," a sign of his celestial intelligence. He takes sustenance from the process and the essence of the sacrifice, rather than from the transitory portion—the physical flesh. Hermes overrides his newly created senses with the consciousness of immortality, and of hierarchy, both external and internal. Despite his unconventional method, the meat flag in the barn signifies his divine rectitude. Hermes is marking himself out as the Magickian of Olympus.

The true magickian is familiar with humility, and this is another trait Hermes exhibits; though never cloying or sycophantic, he is ever-willing to serve the gods and mortals alike. Hermes understands the dignity of service, and the pleasure inherent in being of functional use. Throughout these escapades he retains a sense of immortal perspective, so assured of his own divinity that to serve is a pleasure. He is utilitarian in outlook. At the Hermaea in Crete (the temple to Hermes), masters waited on their feasting slaves, just as, recently, officers waited on soldiers at Christmas during the world wars; an important act of grace and one which the properly trained witch and magickian will instantly recognize.

Hermes often carries a caduceus, the magickal staff comprising two serpents wound about a wand. This (or a version of it) was given to him by Apollo in exchange for the first lyre. The wand, "with which he charms asleep—or, when he wills, awake—the eyes of men," doubles as a shepherd's staff, the guardianship of flocks and herds now being conferred to the wily younger brother. Hermes is characterized by his jaunty broad-rimmed hat, and often wears winged sandals, "ambrosial, golden, that carry him over water and over endless land on a puff of wind," and a helmet which has the power to make him invisible. He is able to transform himself into a breeze or mist in order to pass through keyholes and the like, and is as adept a guide and messenger in the Underworld as in the land of the living.

Although some early representations of Hermes depict him as a bearded man, it is as smooth-skinned *ephebe* that we most often behold him. He is the tricky teenager of Olympia, rather as Artemis is the celestial tomboy. Lithe and agile, Hermes emulates his half-sister's keen eye and steady aim. His magickian aspect allows him to extricate other Olympians from distress, most notably Zeus from imprisonment inflicted by the monster Typhoeus. Thus, Hermes is instrumental in liberating the civilizing influence against the chaotic and elemental powers (represented by the mutant Typhoeus). Typhoeus has cut the tendons of Zeus' hands and feet and trapped him in the dark, rendering him incapable of kinetic action. Hermes restores light, liberty, and the essential tissue, renewing the god's strength. His Houdini aspect, operative in all spheres, provides a cornerstone of Olympian history.

Like most Olympians, Hermes has amorous dalliances, some sources indicate with Persephone, Hecate, and Aphrodite, three of the most interesting and passionate goddesses of any pantheon. Nymphs were also amongst his lovers, probably light relief after the first three. He had children, of course, but is rarely paternal—except in teaching his children tricks. The Homeric Hymn to Pan cites "luck-bringing Hermes" as his father, proud and happy of his baby, despite his unusual features—such as a goat's beard. Hermes retains his youthful preoccupations throughout his liaisons, and is never compromised by overwhelming emotions, as are so many gods and demi-gods, but rather, stays on top of the situation at all times. He is the sort of man who would be described today as "commitment phobic," definitely more one-night-stand material than potential husband. (Though no doubt, when feeling low, one would continually run into him at just the right moment . . .)

First among the gods, Hermes honors beautiful-haired Mnemosyne, "mother of the Muses"; he does so in song, and rivals Apollo with its sweetness. His reverence for the goddess whose name means "memory" indicates his ability to learn through experiment and experience, as well as his eloquence, to which a sharp memory is essential. He forgets nothing, adding to his skills the ability to negotiate in the light of a full knowledge of his opponent's past. This is a skill emulated by all business people, and adds to his relevance in the arena of commerce. In addition to this, Hermes honors Mnemosyne as generatrix of the Muses, a propitious start to any creative endeavor. The nine sisters, whose gifts include singing and dancing, would no doubt hold great appeal to this fun-loving individual. Hermes' mother, Maia, was also said to be "one of their retinue."

Hermes is connected also with the sudden stroke of good fortune, known in Greek as a *hermaion*. Any gain is relevant to this god, especially the return of an entrepreneurial enterprise. He fructifies, partly in conjunction with his pastoral role, partly through good business sense and well-concealed, immaculately directed selfishness. Though capable of rescuing gods and mortals and slaying monsters, Hermes' essential nature is one of seeking individual pleasure. He is a typical Olympian in this sense. His modus operandi is eccentric—indeed, he operates entirely outside the established structure of Olympus, but he belongs to it in soul. He is capable of kindness, certainly, but he stands primarily for a cult of Self. His motivations are acquisition—for the sake of the challenge (he certainly is no hoarder, treating objects as manifestations of the physical for their symbolic value alone, as we have seen in the case of the divine cattle), and pleasure. He is not adverse to bribery to further his causes; in the Homeric Hymn, Hermes is spotted stealing the divine herd by an old man, and tells him, "Surely you will have much wine when these [vines] bear fruit, if you obey me and strictly remember not to have seen what you have seen, and not to have heard what you have heard."

Hermes is associated with Dionysus, having transferred Dionysus as babe from Zeus' thigh to be mothered by his aunt Ino. Later, when Hera's implacable jealousy had driven Ino mad and was threatening the life of Dionysus, Zeus turned the latter into a kid, and Hermes led him again to safety. Boiled seed was offered to both Dionysus and Hermes during Dionysiac festivals and rites. This connection underlines the Arcadian aspect of Hermes.

The vivacious Hermes is also a housebreaker, and fathered Autolycus, on whom he bestowed the ability to make anything he touched become invisible. Thus did Autolycus become the Master Thief. Hermes likewise is the one chosen by the gods to steal Hector's body from the revenge-hungry Achilles, who despite being half-divine is taking his feelings too far in the opinion of most Olympians. It is Hermes who contacts King Priam, Hector's father, with news of the whereabouts of his son's body. This was particularly important in the case of a hero, that he might receive the proper honor and due sacrifices which would alleviate some of his suffering in the Underworld and allow his name to live on in glory. Hermes "lights the way for mortals" in more senses than one; he also delivers directions and brings advice.

Another epithet of Hermes is "the Good Companion," a trait demonstrated at times such as the comforting and protection King Priam as he appeals to Achilles to release his son's body for burial. The understanding between the Achaean hero and the Trojan king, engineered by Hermes, is one of the most touching scenarios of *The Iliad*.

He is also a "good companion" owing to his charming manner. Even Apollo, whose pride has been hurt by Hermes, promises "to love no other among the immortals, neither god nor man sprung from Zeus, better than Hermes." There is doubtless an element of relief in this, for the gushing promise is elicited immediately after Hermes has sworn on the Styx never to steal any of Apollo's effects again.

Hermes' heroic feats include the slaying of Hippolytus, Argus, whom he lulls to sleep with his flute, then kills; and the discovery of Ares, captured by giants, whom he releases "more dead than alive, worn out by the iron chain." The strength of Hermes is obvious from the first; Apollo attempts to bind him with "strong withes" when he is still a babe, "but the bands would not hold him and the withes of the osier fell far from him." Hermes uses his magickal ability to turn Apollo's wrath to his own advantage; for instead of binding Hermes into submission, as his older brother wishes, the withes "quickly grew and covered all the wild-roving cattle by the will of thievish Hermes, so that Apollo was astonished as he gazed."

Hermes is not so much heroic, as a lateral thinker, an exception to every rule. His encoding mind changes the psychological landscape of Greek mythology. Master of duplicity and celestial charmer, Hermes is one of the gods who keeps the spirit of Olympus alive and kicking.

CONTACTING HERMES

The best time to contact Hermes is at the dark of the moon. Wednesday is good, in respect of his mercurial aspect. Candles should be black, red, and silver.

No bath is necessary, but a Tarot or Rune reading beforehand might get you in a suitable mood. Best also to approach him during a busy time in your life; Hermes easily attunes to the "rushing about" vibrations. Do not forget that he especially protects travelers and those on missions.

VISUALIZATION FOR LATERAL THINKING AND CRAFTY SCHEMES

Firstly, establish what your venture is to be. If it is nothing in particular, try to "bundle up" your thoughts into a condensed form which will be easier to present to Hermes later. If you know exactly what you are aiming at, imagine it wrapped in a spotted scarf at the end of a long wand or stick. A caduceus is even better. Now place this staff over your shoulder, and imagine yourself setting out on a journey. Your goal is the place that will allow you to put your plans into action.

As your foot descends, a winding path unravels itself before you. Your foot is shod, you notice, in a cloth shoe with a pointed, curling toe, like that of a medieval jester. Your legs are clad in green stockings, and you wear a dandy tunic. You look, in short, just like the Fool in the Tarot.

You set off with a buoyant step.

After you have spent your initial energy on your upbeat gait and on admiring the natural surroundings, you begin to feel a little fatigued. You had half expected to get there by now—wherever it is you are going. On second thoughts, you are not entirely sure where it was you were aiming for when you set out. Ah well, keep walking, and perhaps it will come back to you.

A few leagues later, and you are getting quite tired. Twilight is descending, and the road seems to be stretching on forever. So much for the lateral thinking you were banking on! Your thoughts seem to be entirely linear, like your walk.

Night falls. You forge forward, but with little light and even less energy. You begin to feel lost and a little afraid. Yet you plod on, determined to see the visualization through, because you know you can.

In the darkness ahead there seems to be a clot of even greater darkness. It looks like black blood coagulated around a vein; several veins. Unnerved and slightly sickened, you force yourself to approach.

You are at a crossroads. The hag goddess Hecate is strong here; a stake topped by a glaring mare marks her presence. You do not wish, however, to invoke the attentions of the wily, murderous crone, and so you sneak past the dark altar, intent on reaching your goal. The problem is, which in which direction does it lie?

There are three paths to chose from now.

Suddenly, what looks like a scarp-slope catches your eye. It seems to glow like golden nuggets in your mind's eye; it marks the path. You instinctively go for the road it is on.

Just as you reach the pillar and its numerous small stones, you feel the presence of a very tall, dark man coming up the road to meet you. As he gets closer you realize that the extra shadow on his face is caused by a hat with a gigantic rim. You dimly perceive him smiling at you through the gloom.

"Are you lost?" he asks, and then, without waiting for an answer; "I can show you the Way."

By now, the thought of further travelling is far from appealing to you. You do not, however, wish to offend the stranger. In fatigue, you thank Hermes and ask him to sit awhile and refresh your senses by talking with you. Hermes readily agrees.

You unpack your bundle of schemes and show it to your bright companion. He assesses it in a trice, and smiles. Visualize him picking through the roots and shoots of your ideas, and pay close attention to which ones he grins at and replaces, and which he casts into the rubble at the base of his devotional pillar.

Converse with him mentally, if you wish, and ask him your questions out straight, if it seems appropriate. He may decide to entertain you with a tale or two himself.

When he has finished, he vanishes in a puff of a mist. You look around, and instantly spot the path you have been seeking. One step, and you are back in your room, your bundle of ideas held firmly in your hand.

Now write down your thoughts on the scheme to hand, including what has been "thrown out" by Hermes, and what remains.

Employ all of your intuition and *nous* to set your plans into action on the material plane.

MUNDANE ARCHETYPES

The Hermes-boy is a charmer, always highly entertaining and mocking of convention, which he can afford to be because he is always accepted by others owing to his easy manner and ready wit. He is not, however, pretentious, though he can be highly innovative. He loves to bring the affected down to earth by playing practical jokes on them; the more solemn or poker-faced the victim, the greater Hermes' ruse. He rarely acts out of spite, but rather from the desire to teach people a positive lesson. He believes in the equality of all and is usually a well-heeled Socialist.

Though attractive to girls with his pretty-boy looks and tricky nature, Hermes always stays one step ahead of the chase. He is not interested in being tied to an ordinary relationship; stagnation is death to him. He is passionate one night, aloof the following day, and, like the Anubis-type, quite commitment phobic. He tends to crop up, however, at just the right mutually convenient moment, and frequently you bump into him by "coincidence."

The Hermes-character also exhibits traits of slyness and cunning; he can be underhand in his dealings and is no stranger to theft, at which he is adept and fearless. His nature veers between its fraternal poles—Apolline and Dionysiac—so that he is controlled and focused one day, and hedonistic the next. However, he maintains a strong sense of self throughout all of his shenanigans, and in no sense requires the approval of others to encourage or justify his modus operandi. The Hermes archetype is a lawbreaker unto himself.

TAROT CARDS
The Fool, The Magician, The World

ZEUS

Zeus reigns upright from his throne of stone, eagle eyes surveying his domain. Transgressors he strikes down, and hosts who murder, and all who practice violence and cruel deeds. He is helped, tells Hesiod, by "thrice ten thousand spirits." Mortals may conclude that mighty Zeus is guardian of Justice in this realm.

    This fearsome god, whose voice is thunder, whose wrath casts deities from their place of grace and sends them hurtling toward some bitter penal isle, is, let the worlds proclaim it once again, far-sighted Zeus. His broad brows ever ponderous, deeper than Poseidon's rich domain, his tree-sized scepter held aloft, eyes alert to curve and curl of subtle female form and ever concupiscent, this mountainous-proportioned king of kings demands his toll from gold-haired goddess, mortal girl, and feeble man alike.

Tremble when you think of him! And do not neglect to offer him the finest portions of the sacrificial meat. For he dictates the Fortunes of a man: his social status, what weight his purse, and his progeny. All that makes life bearable on the plane of sorry mortals is a gift of Zeus. Without his blessing, there is nothing to attain, except a hard life full of toil and an eternity as a hungry wraith in Hades' gloom.

To engender Zeus' favor, work hard, be fair in all your dealings, and honor the gods regularly and with heartfelt humility. Treat your elders with respect and follow marital laws, never forgetting to do as Great Zeus says, and not as he actually does.

Zeus, son of "Crooked Cronos" and Rhea, is King of the Gods and special protector of strangers (a trait emphasized in his later, Roman version, Jove.) He is born, like so many other deities, in secret; Krishna and Horus are but two who share this surreptitious form of nativity. In Zeus' case, the danger springs from Cronos, whose epithet epitomizes his thieving ways. It is Zeus' life he wishes to steal, just as he has stolen his father Uranus' regenerative properties by casting his genitals into the frothing ocean. Following a familiar pattern, the Lord of the Old Régime has heard of a threat to his power in the future, and refuses to countenance it. Like King Herod in much later years, he attempts to assail the threat at its nativity; in this case, by swallowing each of his own infants in turn. In some cases he succeeds, but the grief-stricken Rhea soon learns to substitute her babies with stones. Zeus is saved by this act of cunning, and is sent to a safe refuge. Cronos ends up regurgitating those infants which he has successfully swallowed, and awaiting the inevitable end to his Time.

Although the ruler of the Olympian family and of "wretched mortals" alike, Zeus is primarily a weather god. He finds an easy analogue in the functions of other paternal, thunderous deities such as Indra and Thor. Like these, he is governed by a stormy temperament, and feels no compunction to protect his mortal underlings, though he is swift to punish when we fail to honor him. In Hindu myth Indra is ousted by the love-force Krishna, rather as Christ brought a new influx of personal interaction to aspects of the Jewish faith as popularly construed at that time. In the tales of the Aesir, Baldur, the beautiful youngster beloved of all (except for Loki), represents this energy. However, there is no such equivalent in Greek mythology. Zeus stands unchallenged by his court, creating heroes and destroying them as befits his mood, sending monsters to plague others for revenge or amusement, seducing young women through trickery and force, being nagged by his wife Hera, and hurling thunderbolts at any who displease him, a threat to which even Hera is not immune.

The Homeric, autocratic Zeus offers little to "wretched mortals, who like leaves now flourish, as they eat the fruit of the field, and now fade away lifeless" *(The Iliad)*. This bearded god, still in the prime of his physical strength and mental prowess, has no need of humankind, except as sundry entertainment. The principle of *ate* is sent by Zeus, a metaphorical blindness (personified as the goddess Ate) which causes men, heroes, and gods alike to lose their rationality and commit hasty deeds, usually repented of at leisure. Ate gives strength in battle, but has little else to recommend it. The fact that a hotheaded action was inflicted by a god does not relieve the unhappy perpetrator of either the responsibility or the repercussions. There are numerous examples of this malice at play in tales of the Trojan War, not least the circumstance that caused it; Helen's rash passion for Paris, over which she had no control. In this instance, Aphrodite held the marionette strings, although with Zeus' full approval. Homer presents the Trojan tragedies, so richly described in terms of human (and sometimes immortal) suffering, as a form of entertainment for the gods. The Trojans and the Achaeans are like toy soldiers in a game; and Odysseus' epic voyage back to his kingdom involves pitting his wits against Poseidon and a variety of demi-gods and monsters. Boons might be granted by Athena and Zeus, but they are just as frequently counteracted by new challenges. The epic is a celestial soap opera with an interactive, mutually competitive audience.

Likewise in Aeschylus' *Oresteian Trilogy*, we find Orestes unable to win in a battle between individual gods and their functions. Orestes' mother, Clytemnestra, has slain his father, Agamemnon; it is Apollo's (and therefore Zeus') Will to see vengeance done, particularly as Agamemnon is a king, whose Zeus-given rights as such are often invoked in *The Iliad*. All those in power were under the special aegis of Zeus, and the murder of one of these could not go unattended. Consequently, Orestes is commanded to kill his mother. However, there are deities whose special purpose is to punish those who commit matricide—the ghastly Eumenides, or Furies (formerly known as the Erinyes; renamed by Athena at the end of the Oresteian myth)—and Orestes' crime will be twice that of his mother because he will be spilling his own family's blood. So, Orestes may either risk the wrath of Apollo and Zeus, or be perpetually tortured by the Erinyes. The *Mythic Tarot* illustrates this dilemma to a tee, employing the Oresteian tragedy for the suit of Swords. A stern Apollo on one side, whose terrible wrath we have already explored; the fearsome Furies on the other, jabbing at him with their haunting thoughts. His only choice is to act in accordance with the law of Apollo and Zeus—which he does. Eventually, Athena takes pity on the tragic hero and offers respite from the bitter sisters' jibbing; but not until Orestes has suffered greatly.

It is worth noting that the Erinyes evince a moral right in this scenario. Naturally, Clytemnestra is also at fault, having killed her husband, particularly as he arrived victorious back from Ilium, but the fact is, Orestes has killed his mother. No matter what the provocation, all societies and morally aware individuals agree that matricide is wrong. Zeus stands above the question of ethics; indeed, is immune to it at all times. His only concern is that a personal favorite has been wronged, and he cares not what happens to the dispatcher of his own form of justice. It simply Must Be Done.

The Decree of Zeus was often delivered by his messenger Hermes, by the intervention of other gods such as Apollo, or as thunder, the latter providing a handy theatrical device. In Sophocles' *Oedipus at Colonus* for example, "Louder peals the volley of God's thunder" as the play reaches its tragic climax. The sky is described as "ablaze with God's artillery"— note, "God's," not "the Gods." Here Zeus is supreme overlord, epitome of all the powers of all the gods. As their figurehead, he represents all the power of taboo that the unwitting Oedipus has broken, and the vengeance which is ever pending and inflicted.

The Olympians feel no compunction to be overly concerned about mortal men; for why should they? On Mount Olympus they live as perpetually youthful, beautiful gods, perfectly capable of mutual entertainment; involvement with men is a mere frippery. The gods are eternal, whereas human life ends in the blink of an eye. It must indeed have been depressing for those of Homer's mindset, for believing as he purports to, they had nothing to look forward to but a life blighted by the Fates (led by Zeus as *Moriagetes*), and an eternity as a blood-craving wraith in the gloomy Halls of Hades.

Despite the obvious connections with rain and wind, fire is the major elemental attribute of Zeus. In some philosophies we find a loftier Zeus than the Homeric version; here, he becomes the all-pervading element of pure reason. In the work of Empedocles we find Zeus representing fire, Hera air, Aidoneus earth, and Nestis water. Empedocles believed the cosmos to be comprised of these four elements—a concept which will be familiar to the Wiccan and magickian—and that the states of life and death are merely differing combinations of these elements. It is refreshing to discover Zeus operating in this highly spiritual context, which bears a remarkable resemblance to Hindu and Buddhist conceit:

> *And these elements never cease changing place continually, now being all united by Love into one, now each borne apart by the hatred engendered of Strife, until they are brought together in the unity of the all, and become subject to it.*

(Empedocles, c. 493–433 B.C.E., *On Nature*)

Here, Zeus develops a new divine personality; one infinitely more recognizable to us today as godlike. In the same way that the ether, Zeus' domain, infiltrates and surrounds everything, so too does Zeus' omnipotence saturate both the heavenly and earthly realms. We discover that a spiritualized Zeus is capable of love as well as cruelty, and that he may be perceived in this aspect. Thus his progression into more "Jovial" attributes—the welcoming, protective, nurturing god.

In general, however, Zeus' role is far from mystical. He is a monotheistic dictator, often dignified and kindly, true, but barely the ideal deity. His palace stands at the center of Olympus, surrounded by the abodes of the other gods, constructed by the metalsmith and carpenter Hephaestus. Here he abides, Zeus the All-Powerful, worshipped and feared, contemplatively accepting as offerings the smoke of prize rams and oxen sent up by men. Aeschylus describes him as "most perfect of the Blessed Ones, most perfect might among the Perfect, blissful Zeus" (*Supplices*, 524–6). However, the same author is our major source of the Promethean myth, in which Prometheus steals fire from the gods in order to help mankind, and is hideously punished by Zeus for attempting to extricate mortals from their god-inflicted sufferings. If Prometheus is the martyr-hero as Krishna is to Indra and Christ to Yahweh, he certainly is not rewarded for his troubles, as are those others. His torture is eternal, a constantly renewed liver offering itself to the beak of an eagle (Zeus' anthropomorphic bird form), while Prometheus remains tied to a rock. In *Prometheus Bound*, it is categorically declared that, "No one is free but Zeus." Few martyrdoms could be worse than Prometheus'; because it is endless. Prometheus' only comfort is that the gift of fire will remain with men, and that civilization has been initiated by his gift. (Luckily, in one version at least, he is rescued by Herakles later on.) Prometheus is one of the few Greek characters to show compassion to those who are not related to him by blood. He certainly outweighs Zeus in this capacity.

Like Apollo, Zeus is a keen lover, though one infinitely more successful in his amorous endeavors than his effete son. In Hesiod, Metis, "supreme in Wisdom," was his first wife, on whom he sired Athena. However, in a similar manner to Cronos, Zeus was warned that if he maintained his relationship with this all-knowing goddess, he would be ousted by his own offspring. Subsequently he followed in the family tradition and swallowed the problem; this time, mother included. Thus was Athena borne of his cranium, while Metis remained embodied by him, wisdom controlled and encapsulated. Zeus' "forethought" thereby became unsurpassable.

Themis was the next in line, (her name meaning "moral law"), who bore him, amongst others, the Horae (Seasons) and Moerae (Fates). These offspring are particularly relevant to Themis' other role; that of earth. Zeus, the sky god, uniting with Themis, the earth, creates the atmospheric phenomena of the seasons. We witness the transition of a simple sky and weather god into one who is both wise, and "married to Order," environmental and legislative. The genesis of an all-powerful deity is at hand.

There are many other loves in Zeus' legends, but the most significant and durable is Hera, generally accepted as his permanent celestial counterpart. It is "Hera of the golden sandals" who watches her husband with as many eyes as are harbored by her peacocks' tails, who rebukes and soothes him, stands by him and plots behind his back, and essentially has an entertainingly human relationship with him. The "henpecked husband" scenarios evident in *The Iliad*, for example, recall the experiences of many men (perhaps creating a more personal attitude to the god), and also other deities, such as Siva with Parvati. In both instances, however, the nagging is clearly justified—carousing with other women, for example—while both gods claim that their superior positions render them immune to such mundane considerations as infidelity. A familiar male attitude indeed!

Hera exacts a terrible revenge on many of Zeus' lovers, especially those who are mortal. Io was transformed into a heifer by Zeus to conceal her from Hera, but the latter spied her out and sent a stinging gadfly to pursue and torture her. Semele was goaded by Hera into asking her lover to appear in his full glory before her—a wish which Zeus reluctantly granted, killing Semele instantly. Her mortal vessel was too fragile to withstand the sudden influx of divinity revealed and unleashed by Zeus.

These and countless other affairs meant that Zeus was rich in children. He fathered hundreds of young Olympians and demi-gods, assuring himself an enthusiastic following. He ruled over all, and blessed those in power. The Greeks often used the word "Zeus" as a prefix as we might say "king." The king was, of course, his figurehead on earth, and worldly power and favor his god-given gifts.

CONTACTING ZEUS

Obviously, with the thunderbolt and lightning as his special weapons, the best time to attune to Zeus is just before or during a storm. At the very least, pick a dark rainy day.

A thunderstorm is a powerful scenario for any magickal working— rarely is the atmosphere so conducive to visualization and conductivity. However, we have to be careful to work with the natural currents without becoming overwhelmed by them—either literally or metaphorically. It is easy to be overawed by such phenomena, or to fall into the opposite camp and adopt a megalomaniac stance. This is a very real danger when working with one such as Zeus.

Be sure to keep yourself and your aims in perspective during this visualization and lateral workings. You are not meant to rule the world, you do not wish to be a dictator; you are merely requesting from a power much greater than our own, in this instance represented by Zeus, that you be given enough "of what it takes to get along." Zeus, like all gods, is a priest of the Great Cosmic Intelligence; and his particular brand of energy is volatile, so be warned. A good dose of respect and humility combined with a natural sense of self-worth should keep you in balance while working with this stentorian deity.

Visualization for Strength and Power in the Earthly Realm

To reiterate, this visualization is not intended to facilitate an ego trip. It is intended to give the necessary means to those who require status and power in order to achieve their positive, humanitarian ends. It will also give the power of leadership to its successful operator.

Candles, if you wish to use them, should be gray, purple, and black. Incense should be thick and savory, such as copal, once considered a "food of the gods." (Admittedly Mexican rather than Greek, but a handy substitute for burnt animal flesh!)

Visualize yourself standing on a mound at the center of a flat, desolate earth. Above you, the clouds swirl like bitter sea currents, every shade of gray from white to rain-heavy black. The "ponderous black brows" of Zeus are frowning heavily on the land, as he wonders what this speck of mortality down below is doing making itself known to him.

As you feel the lightning flash of Zeus' awareness shattering your complacency, begin to petition the Father of Gods on your own behalf. Visualize your intended campaign, and make it seem as exciting as possible, an entertaining and meaningful strategy which will bring great glory in its accomplishment.

Send this concept very strongly and steadily into the storm god's open mind, riding its powerful currents as best you can.

It will not take you long to perceive Zeus' reaction to your supplication. The symbolism of his response is unlikely to be subtle; you should have no problem interpreting the conclusion to your visualization.

When you have attained your answer, thank Zeus and return to your temple or room. You do not want to bore him with your mosquito-like drone. With any luck, he will have invested you with all the energy you require to fulfill your purpose.

If you do not feel inspired and fortified at this juncture, reconsider your ideas. They may be ill conceived or unrealistic. Once you have reformulated your ideas, you could always try again.

VISUALIZATION FOR FORCEFULNESS

This sounds like an unusual exercise to find in a book that intends to foster desirable traits and experiences; however, there are times when force, even brute force, is required. In Qabalistic terms, this is represented by Geburah, which counterbalances merciful Chesed. Without Geburah's ability to cauterize, growth would get out of control and deteriorate into destruction. On a microcosmic level, a generous nature can often become burdened as more and more unreasonable demands are made of it. It can take a little "brute force" to enable the self-made martyr to extricate him or herself from the situation.

There are other times when force is needed; a teacher who cannot control his or her pupils is useless, and often it takes a thunderous voice, at the very least, to facilitate this. Alternately, a relationship may require that a foot be put down. Whatever the situation, Zeus is the ideal deity to whom to apply for the strength and ability to command, sometimes jovially, sometimes ruthlessly, in whatever way is needed.

Imagine yourself at the top of a mountain. Above your head is nothing but the black empyrean, starry and teeming with the consciousness of the gods. Your head is above gravity level, and feels light as a feather, though your breathing is deep, aspirational. Your body remains on earth, though high above its normal habit, and you have a perfect overview of your life.

It is a clear day, and beneath you sweeps the landscape of your situation. Everything you see down there, diminutive though it is, bespeaks the circumstances that have driven you to perform this visualization. Even though the symbols look small from above, you feel attached to them still. Indeed, on looking, you can see fine lines of silvery light connecting you with each one.

From this vantage point, it is possible to imagine how your require-ments might actually be made to affect the situation. Tug at a string a lit-tle; see how you can move the object or person at the end of it to and fro, dragging them hither and thither if you so desire. This must be how the gods feel about everything, all of the time.

Now, concentrate on exactly what it is that you wish to achieve. Do you want to change things around, facilitating your own ideas, altering the circumstances you see below you? Or do you wish to make your feel-ings and thoughts known to the other person or people concerned? Pos-sibly, both.

When you are clear in your mind as to what you desire, and how to symbolize this using the objects at the end of your silver strings, you are ready to begin.

Take one very deep inhalation, and raise your right arm toward the heavens as you do. Mentally connect with Zeus. As you exhale, feel his thunderous, shocking energy flowing into your arm, despotic and all-powerful. It vibrates with a silver-black light and a low rumble. Your arm feels heavy with it, and almost scorched. You wish to dispel it swiftly.

Now return your inner vision to the symbolic scene far below you, and dispatch your power as you see fit. Destroy the obstacles which stand in your way—they are easy to incinerate from up here—and use some of your energy to bless the other humans concerned with a lightning bolt of awareness of you. Do not desist until the scene beneath you is exactly as you wish it to be.

When you have finished this part of the exercise, thank Zeus for lend-ing you this tiny splinter of his energy, and get ready to put it into action on the outer plane.

This exercise is best performed just before you broach a confrontation. As you face your "opponent," be sure to visualize your entire body full of the silver-black storm energy of despotic Zeus. As previously mentioned, this may be used to great effect in standing up for one's rights, refusing to be a doormat, finally being listened to, etc. It is inappropriate to use any of these techniques for selfish or harmful purposes; magick always returns to burn the fingers of its wrongful perpetrator. However, if your cause is just and you simply require a bit of strength and prestige to get your point across, Zeus should be willing to oblige.

If your situation proves particularly tricky, there are methods of defense you may use, such as envisaging the harmful energies of your opponents bouncing off your coat of astral armor; and methods of attack, such as visualizing your statements as bolts of lightning, and mentally projecting them as such into the mind of the other party. When working with Zeus, do not be afraid to get angry; it can be well directed, particularly if you have given the matter a lot of forethought.

Essentially, Zeus is no fan of the underling—only the most heroic catch his eye—so it is important to really make the effort for yourself rather than relying on gods to do it for you. Together, however, you may prevail. Do not forget—your opinion is as valid as anyone else's. You have the right to be heard, so let your thoughts be known. And as you do so, let your energy flow. That is what the greatest of the gods always do.

Mundane Archetypes

Zeus is the typical Victorian patriarch. He rules his family with a rod of iron, and the lives of its individual members revolve around him or in accordance with his wishes. Intelligent, obedient girls of plain aspect and feisty boys will please him; other of his children will be marginalized by his gigantic ego.

Zeus loves his creature comforts, particularly food, which tends to be of the more traditional ilk. Roast meats are among his favorite, along with sweet cakes and biscuits. He is nearly always of larger size around the midriff.

Like his bigger archetype, the microcosmic Zeus crackles with fury and sends thunderous shockwaves of (often unreasonable) anger throughout his homestead when crossed. He evinces everything typical of a Leo male at his worst.

There was a time when many families had a Zeus at their nucleus. A civilization designed to create simpering females had allowed the male psyche to remain undisciplined and self-indulgent, so that often, a forty-year-old man had all the psychological finesse of a three-year-old boy. The hierarchical mind of this archetype leads it to believe itself at the top of the pecking order for reasons such as gender, physical size, social status, and job. Finances are a key to this man's power struggle; if he has dependants, they will constantly be reminded of the fact. If his resources are low, he will use other bludgeons such as physical strength. He is keen to punish those who go against his will, an he can often degenerate into a bully and wife-beater.

I am not naïve enough to suggest that times have changed so much that Zeus has handed over his mantle to Hera, but there are fewer of him around in the West than there were even in the 1980s. The Chinese, however, are creating a whole new society of Zeus', by pampering and indulging their only sons so much that they are commonly referred to by all as the "Little Emperors." One pities the girl who will one day have to become his empire. In this hemisphere, some who would, in a conducive environment, have been Zeus, are easing into postfeminist alternatives, and are becoming more like Ra and Osiris, sun gods who have had their day.

In his positive aspects, Zeus can, of course, be great company: warm, expansive, and hospitable. He is often popular and respected by his peers. He usually treats those outside his family with more attention to their feelings than those in it. He seems not to respect the personal feelings of his own progeny, though he is proud of their achievements.

He may be inclined to have extramarital affairs. Even if he does not, Zeus will inevitably accuse his wife of doing so. His fiery nature makes him possessive and volatile, and his acute awareness of his status causes him some paranoia. Public humiliation is the worst thing in the world to this arrogant archetype.

Tarot cards
The Emperor, King of Swords

DIONYSUS

The wise fool is riding into town on his donkey.

Wild-eyed, flush-cheeked, word of his arrivals spreads through the town like a fast-growing vine. Flagons hang on either side of his mount, emanating bright visions even before drunk. Flowers and figs flourish an abundant pollen-filled fanfare. The gathering crowds are beginning to feel a little tipsy just by breathing the same air as the beautiful youth. Girls giggle in clusters. Warm air caresses their skins.

One or two of the men attempt to assail the stranger; who dares to cause such a stir in this respectable dwelling place? Dionysus, his face a mask of perfect sweetness, turns them into stone.

At the sight of this, people shake their heads in wonder and the mood heightens to the color of their blood. The girls are laughing now, gazing goggle-eyed on the succulent god, running their hands over their hips and breasts, beginning to see light increasing in the atmosphere, a cross-reference of dimensions. The mountains of Olympia shimmer where once was open sky; they blink, and it is gone.

"Cast off your clothes!" shrieks one of the women, and the girls tear their dresses in abandonment. Dionysus, amused, replaces their garb with fawn and panther skins, and they grab at ivy, everywhere increasing, and place it in their hair.

A woman holds a drum, and beats it to the rhythm of their mood. Ever-increasing in speed, circling around them and infiltrating their bodies, they begin to follow Dionysus. He is heading out of town.

Sunshine pours like hot honey over the Arcadian bower. The mood ferments; soon they are abandoned in ambrosial amnesia, some reveling, others dancing, while the great god Dionysus runs amok, now a bull, now a lion, now an adolescent let loose in his parent's abandoned home. As he moves, they feel themselves enhanced through him, his electricity pumping through their bodies, connected by their mystic ecstasy.

He holds aloft a horn, and all drink from it. Their lips now red as blood, eyes rolling back like those of frightened horses— and yet they know no fear—the Maenads froth at the mouth and form a pack with which to implement their next move.

In one version of the myth, Dionysus is the son of Persephone by Zeus. However, according to Hesiod, Dionysus' mother is Semele, a mortal. Semele is naturally the subject of Hera's uxorial wrath. To punish her for causing Zeus to be unfaithful, Hera persuades Semele to ask her lover to appear before her "in all his glory." Hera sows the seeds of doubt in the innocent girl's mind, suggesting that her lover might really be some kind of monster, hoping to destroy the pleasure of their union.

Knowing that she will be unable to withstand his unveiled resplendence, Zeus attempts to dissuade her, but Semele is adamant. As Hera had planned, and as Zeus had feared, the splendor of the King of the Gods is too much for Semele's mortal vessel, and she dies instantly. Like a low-watt light bulb during a power surge, Dionysus' mother's circuits are blown.

A barrier of ivy springs up and protects Dionysus from the celestial fire. Zeus rescues his embryonic son from Semele's body and places Dionysus in his own thigh to gestate, hence one of Dionysus' epithets, "*Twice Born*." The young god comes to represent excess—a principle which, even before birth, he is able to withstand. Apart from anything, he is able to improvise. His paternity makes him strong, and he is twice-infused with celestial energy; first genetically, and then when Semele is exposed to Zeus.

Hera's wrath is relentless, however, and she causes Dionysus' guardians, his aunt Ino and her husband Athamas, to go insane. Hermes rescues the child and carries him to Mount Nysa, where he is looked after by the nymphs, and educated by the drunken but wisdom-filled Silenus, and the Muses and satyrs.

Dionysus is the god of wine and revelry. One of his titles is "Loud-crying Dionysus." As this appellation suggests, he represents the wild side of our natures and personalities; unbridled inspiration, throwing protocol (and law and order) to the winds, and, rather like Pan, indulging in sensuality. It is in this way that he differs from Apollo, with whom he is continually contrasted by post-Nietzchean writers. Both gods confer inspiration, but Apollo's is healing and creative in a structured sense, while that of Dionysus is revealing and destructive. Like Siva in his death-dance, Dionysus and his worshippers come tumbling down the mountainside intoxicated and hungry for *sparagmos,* a flesh-tearing frenzy. This highly theatrical trait is used to chilling effect in Euripides' tragedy *The Bacchae.*

Dressed in his fawn or panther skin and bearing aloft his *thyrsus,* a staff topped by a pine cone (or occasionally double-pronged) and festooned with living ivy, Dionysus traveled a great deal, taking wine with him, rewarding the gracious host with vine-stock, and punishing the less gracious with madness. Like Silenus, he is associated with the donkey, and in some accounts, rides on one. He is said to have frightened the Olympian giants with the harsh braying of his steed. He is the wise fool who cares not how he appears to others, fully conscious, like Hermes, of his innate and all-encompassing divinity, even in madness.

Dionysus' loves were various; in some cases he succeeded in seducing them, in others he had to be content with the typical Olympian revenge of transforming the errant party into a tree. He also enjoys the art of petrifaction, often turning those who displease him into rocks.

Dionysus does, however, marry Ariadne after she has been abandoned by Theseus. In the Homeric version, this occurs after Ariadne's death through Artemis, connecting Dionysus with the idea of the afterlife, with which he is not usually associated.

The Homeric Hymn to Dionysus tells a curious tale. As a "stripling youth," Dionysus is kidnapped by pirates for an intended ransom. Only the helmsman recognizes in the smiling, dark-eyed young man, "his rich dark hair waving about him," and on his "strong shoulders . . . a purple robe," the hallmark of divinity. He bids the other pirates let the boy-god go, for even their strong bonds cannot hold him (just as those of Hermes unraveled themselves when Apollo tried to bind him). However, they refuse, and, god held captive aboard, they hoist sail.

As soon as they are on their way, "strange things" start to happen. Dionysus causes wine, the liquid most sacred to him, to flow throughout the ship, accompanied by "a heavenly smell." It is interesting to note in the context of Dionysiac phenomena that wonderful aromas often precede epileptic attacks, which are connected in many cultures to elevated and shamanic states. They induce the sort of behavior that would be perfectly at home in the retinue of Dionysus.

Living vines begin to grow and flourish in the ship. With his habitual excess, Dionysus adds to the flowers berries, and then festoons the ship with elaborate garlands. Even when he is set adrift in the sterile sea, Dionysus' fecund, vivifying qualities are irrepressible.

At the sight of these miracles, the pirates relent and attempt to return to dry land, but by now, the young god whom they dared to disrespect is angry. He shape-shifts into a lion, a symbol of his regal status and solar aspect, quite different to that of his equally solar brother Apollo. Dionysus fertilizes, Apollo enlightens. They are different aspects of the same life-giving star, brothers, yet light-years apart. Dionysus' choice of the lion-form emphasizes their unity. Likewise the bear, sacred to Apollo's twin, Artemis, which Dionysus creates "amidships," in order to demonstrate "his wonders."

In lion form, Dionysus then lunges for the master of the pirate ship. His sailors are forced to fling themselves off the ship in order avoid the bloodthirsty wrath of Dionysus. They are changed mercifully into dolphins, again expressing a connection with Apollo, to whom dolphins are sacred. Perhaps this represents Dionysus' Apolline decision to control his wrath. In only killing the captain who ordered his imprisonment in the first instance, Dionysus is indeed acting reasonably. Apollo or Artemis in the same situation would probably have shot each and every one of the crew for their hubris. Indeed, Dionysus goes on to comfort the helmsman who had advised his mates to release the god, blessing him with the words, "You have found favor with my heart."

This depiction of Dionysus bears a stark contrast to his representation in Euripides' *The Bacchae*. In this play, the punishment of King Pentheus, who has disrespected him (admittedly in a more headstrong manner than the pirates) and spied on his Maenads, is to be torn limb from limb by the Bacchic revelers, including his own mother, whose eyes roll and who foams at the mouth. It is not until the religious frenzy leaves her that she realizes, most horribly, what she has done. Unfortunately this means that the devout are punished along with the blasphemer, for both Pentheus' mother and grandfather have given due honor to Dionysus, but are destroyed by the fate of their cynical relative.

The cult of Dionysus may perhaps be summarized by this quotation from *The Bacchae:*

> *Blest is the happy man*
> *Who knows the mysteries the gods ordain,*
> *And sanctifies his life,*
> *Joins soul with soul in mystic unity,*
> *And, by due ritual made pure,*
> *Enters the ecstasy of mountain solitudes;*
> *Who observes the mystic rites*
> *Made lawful by Cybele the Great Mother;*
> *Who crowns his head with ivy,*
> *And shakes aloft his wand in worship of Dionysus.*

The first four lines refer to the mystical state of union with the god—what we would call "self-realization," which is possible on the Dionysiac path. "Joins soul with soul in mystic unity" has a distinctly Christian ring to it, though, of course, it was written about five hundred years before the birth of Christ. The reason it sounds so familiar is that it expresses the concept of a personal religion; of individual interaction with spiritual concepts and with God. This contrasts greatly with the Homeric attitude of three hundred years earlier, an attitude in which Apollo and Zeus are rooted; that of the gods as lofty and mortals "lowly" and irrelevant. Perhaps it is due to the bulk of our information on Apollo and Zeus being Homeric that we perceive them in this manner. Dionysus is peripheral at this point.

However, there can be no doubt that Dionysus, like Demeter, Persephone, and to some extent Orpheus, was approached on this very modern-seeming, personal level. This is precisely the sort of spirituality that the hippie movement of the 1960s attempted to reclaim from the Apolline (as in, knowledge received, not perceived) 1950s. Life is indeed then "sanctified," as one ceases to be one of a million and becomes one *in* a million, with a sense of personal import coupled, most significantly, with an awareness of the Creative Intelligence facilitated by its aspect or representative, the demi-god.

This idea of a personal rapport with God which counters conventional expectations—the rites being orgiastic, women who worship Dionysus abandoning their homes and roaming the mountains—is reminiscent of Krishna worship, in which, in mythological terms at least, women hear the call of his flute and abandon all household duties to be with him. Both gods challenge the mundane with a promise of meaningful ecstasy. Both gods whirl their partners in dance in a rural setting. We are reminded of the Dervish route to ecstasy. The tearing of living flesh in the case of the Bacchantes is an extreme form of Eucharist, and marks the transition of power of the god into their physical and mental bodies. He has, of course, already infused them on other levels. This is a solidifying ritual, the equivalent of a witch saying, "So mote it Be," and closing the Circle.

"And by due ritual made pure"; Dionysus' excess is part of a carefully controlled operation. Despite appearances to the contrary, it is not random or chaotic, but a deliberate inducement of a particular state, characterized by Apolline scientific precision. The "mountain solitude" is not to be defiled by city concerns. It is a place of wildness and natural impulse, and it is actually the influence of Apollo and other civic gods (such as Athena) of which Dionysus' supplicant is being cleansed. There must be a balance between the City and the Country; both have their protective gods and their deliberately set boundaries. So too with human nature, with its important mental abilities, rationale, and ability to think in terms of society at large; but then the equally essential ability to think laterally and creatively, express the instinctual urge, and be selfishly free, at least once in a while. Without this, we become doormats of the Greater Good.

"Made lawful by the Great Mother Cybele." Here we have the opposite of Athena/Artemis; the thunder-thighed great Mamma, pure animal female, in whose presence all rationale is lost, and instinct and basic need rule the day. Cybele represents Nature "red in tooth and claw." Dionysus is said to have been initiated into her mysteries at Phyrgia, and these account for some of the more harrowing aspects of his worship, which is known to have included the immolation of boys, human sacrifice, flagellation, and, of course, sparagmos. Seen at its most elevated, this partaking of live flesh while in a state of divine inebriation is an early Eucharist. The wine which flows from Dionysus, the sharing of the flesh of a slain god (or representative thereof), contains the formula for the Christian transubstantiation. Dionysus grafts a mystical dimension onto the cult of Cybele, the most primitive of Greek godforms, and adds artistry to she who stands out amongst them as the least aesthetically pleasing, least appropriate to a pantheon. However, as archetypal chthonic woman, she deserves and receives the respect of Dionysus and his followers.

The ivy wreath mentioned in the following line is the hallmark of the Bacchante. Unlike laurel, its Apolline counterpart, ivy grows wild and fast, clinging to other forms of life and often suffocating them. When inspired (or intoxicated), the Dionysiac has a similar disregard for its fellow beings. It climbs, relentlessly, towards union with God. It does not stop to worry over ethical issues. Its actions are sacred, for the ritual purity conferred beforehand liberates it from mundane concerns. I say "it," incidentally, rather than "him or her," because of the dehumanizing effect of the Bacchic frenzy. The sacred animal state leaves little room for scruple in the depersonalized mind of the devotee.

The wand that is "shaken aloft" epitomizes the forward-forging, fertilizing properties of Dionysus. In the Tarot, the Ace of Wands, Dionysus' Trump, signifies abundance, creativity, and communication. These are among the gifts that the wine god can confer. Also, sudden changes which are of import to the querent.

Dionysus certainly has a Pan-like element of the sudden and unexpected about him. Pan is a close associate of Dionysus', and one who represents Dionysus' ithyphallic aspect. As a god of vegetation, believed by the Phrygians of Thrace to be bound in winter, freed in summer, and as an all-round fecund godform, Dionysus requires this aspect to be symbolized somewhere in his retinue. He, as child or dark-eyed youth, does not bear it himself, but the male generative property is amply demonstrated by the Sileni and satyrs in his crew, as well as by Priapus and Pan. Dionysus' electrifying adrenaline-rushes are delivered on the subtle planes, and are closer to madness than those of any other deity. In being associated with the unpredictable, he is typical of the gods, but the ability to shock is a province of the Arcadian rather than civic deities at this point (nowadays, of course, the roles are reversed!) In Euripides' "Helen," the Chorus exclaims:

> *The gods reveal themselves in many forms,*
> *Bring many matters to surprising ends.*
> *The things we thought would happen did not happen;*
> *The unexpected god makes possible. . . .*

The unexpected is exactly what Dionysus, like Pan, is all about.

As Apollo and Dionysus are so often used to express contrasting states and situations—logical versus irrational, civic versus Arcadian, evolution versus natural—it is worth noting some of their many similarities.

As sons of Zeus and citizens of Olympus, both evince the properties, typical of the gods, of being beautiful, ever-youthful, and inspirational. Apollo gives inspiration through knowledge received; by his Pythias and priests, who in turn interpret and impart their prophecies and omens to the supplicant. Dionysus gives inspiration through knowledge perceived; with no intercessors, his devotees become "possessed" of the god, and have a direct experience of divinity. Both gods heal; Apollo directly, and through revoking his wrath or that of the other gods (such as when the Greek army is spared after Apollo has received due reparation for the insult to his priest in *The Iliad)*; and Dionysus through drink and subsequent amnesia. This ability is summed up in *The Bacchae*, when Teiresias comments: "When mortals drink their fill/Of wine, the sufferings of our unhappy race/Are banished, each day's troubles are forgotten in sleep."

In a similar vein, in Egyptian myth, Sekhmet is tricked into forgetting to destroy mankind by getting drunk on what looks like blood (or wine), and falling asleep. Dionysus is a sleep bringer and, as anyone who has ever suffered excess of alcohol will know, herald of amnesia.

Apollo and Dionysus are equally solar. Both have a pastoral aspect and can increase flocks and crops (Apollo is responsible for pest control, and is often perceived as a shepherd). Apollo operates through light and air/gas (he shoots his arrows through it, and his priestesses are made eloquent by laurel smoke and possibly gaseous emissions in the case of Delphi—though some sources claim to have disproved this point), and Dionysus through warmth and moisture; light and liquid. Sunshine on the vine makes wine.

Further to the solar correspondences, though Apollo with his golden hair is more obvious a candidate than dark-locked Dionysus, the latter has, as already noted, the lion as his primary animal form. It might also be said that, while Apollo represents light, Dionysus is warmth. Alcohol is, of course, renowned for its warming properties. Both are essential properties of a life-giving star.

Sunlight is purifying. It destroys bacteria and heals many diseases. Apollo is famed for his art of purification; he presides over lustral baths and ritual cleansing. Dionysus too requires and facilitates purity before his sacred groves and hillsides are visited by the Bacchic revelers. As stated in *The Bacchae*, it is necessary to be "by due ritual made pure" before entering the "ecstasy of mountain solitudes."

Through ecstasy, Dionysus expands. Rule-bringing Apollo defines and contains.

Both gods are fluent in musical art; Apollo is renowned for his beautiful voice and skill on the lyre, while Dionysus has in his retinue Pan, whose syrinx is played with love and to enchanting effect. Drums were, with their shamanic properties and ability to induce trance states, were used in relation to Dionysus. Rhythmic instruments such as the *tympanon* (a shallow-framed drum) were used to accompany mystery rites, and these encompass without doubt the worship the god of mystic frenzy.

Finally, along with all of their Olympian counterparts, both gods demand worship and punish the infidel. Ironically, though Dionysus is a god of excess while Apollo advertises self-control, there is little to choose between them when it comes to revenge. If anything, Dionysus exercises greater restraint (such as the Homeric example already given) than his brother Apollo in, say, the slaying of Niobe's children.

Essentially, it is important to worship all of the gods—or, as we might say today, to honor all facets of the psyche. We can see what happens when Dionysus (and Aphrodite) are denied, by looking at the Puritans and Victorians and the dreadful, diseased thought-processes and practices which grew out of their strict, unbending discipline. As Blake put it, "Unacted desires breed pestilence in the mind." This does not mean acting on every whim or perverse impulse, but rather, allowing a little space and leeway in which our Dionysiac side might find expression. In Qabalistic terms, this means concentrating on Netzach, the Sephirah of freedom, love, and creativity, as well as on the more disciplined Sephiroth (such as Hod, the sphere of disciplined learning and action which counterbalances Netzach).

Dionysus represents the will to break free of the bonds and enjoy life in whatever way we feel inclined. He allows us to let go—something even the strongest of us require from time to time; to "let rip" for the sake of our sanity. He represents necessary madness.

Thus it is that, despite Apollo's acclaimed musical talent, or ability to elicit something sweet from life, it is said of Dionysus: "He who forgets you can in no wise order sweet song."

CONTACTING DIONYSUS

The best time to connect with Dionysiac energy is when the moon is full, especially in spring. Whenever the world seems to be going mad, and logic is tenuous, Dionysus is around. If you are female, pick a time when your hormones are high, such as when you have PMS. As with

Hecate (see *Invoke the Goddess*), your mood-swings and peculiar, heightened emotions can be used to your advantage.

Needless to say, a few glasses of wine (especially red) will help immensely in contacting Dionysus. There is no getting around the fact that he is the god of alcoholic revelry. An alternative for teetotallers is meditating until you reach a state of "divine inebriation." This is very much a mood thing, and unless you are particularly accomplished in yogic techniques, probably not available "on tap."

A rural setting is the preferable scenario, and, as with Pan, the wilder the better. However, unlike Pan, Dionysus is "available" in the city; the key is excess and excitement.

For a practical approach to Dionysus, visit a funfair and take a roller-coaster ride. The heights and troughs of this adrenal joyride will lead to a state from which a Dionysiac experience would become possible. You might try taking the ride, and then meditating. Likewise, try a bungee-jump; the ultimate Dionysiac sport.

Visualization for Meaningful Pleasure and "Necessary Madness"

The pleasure conferred by Dionysus is applicable to two levels. In its most basic form it is mere physical revelry of the "wine, women, and song" ilk. It brings down empires, the Roman being an obvious example. However, in its developed form it raises the consciousness of its participants/initiates, creating a situation of Eucharist, or communion with the Divine. As Sir George Trevelyan points out in *A Vision of the Aquarian Age,* while the Roman Empire drank and ate itself into extinction, "In the catacombs, a new seed impulse began to blossom, which shook the world. . . . Every wintry decline is an occasion for the bursting of a new spring."

This principle is entirely Dionysiac. From ruin comes new life; from new life comes excess and decline. Dionysus helps slide a place or a situation into decrepitude so that it can be rehabilitated, resurrected. He represents it at the height of its debauchery—though, of course, the definition of debauchery is subjective. To most civilized people, allowing one's senses and sense to be overcome by drink, drugs, or the sex impulse is unacceptable; and this is what Dionysus does. He facilitates a state that can be mystical, opening the eyes of his initiates to the nature of cycles and a sense of belonging and, most importantly, immortality in the cosmos. A common Dionysiac experience is that of being "integrally linked with everything," and perceiving the equality of all life forms. Obviously, in its most extreme forms, Dionysiac energy can provoke scenes revolting to the civilized mind. We certainly plan to avoid tearing other humans (or animals) to death with our hands in (or outside) this visualization!

Imagine yourself sitting in a bar or pub with friends. As you chat, you become aware that the conversation is incredibly mundane. Yes, you are talking about people you all know, and yes, about shared experiences in the past, but what does it all mean, at the end of the day? Absolutely nothing.

You realize that you are bored. Your friends seem stuck in a rut, mindlessly repeating the same old tales, with no new energy or experience to add. You gaze glumly into the bottom of your wine or beer glass, feeling not in the least inebriated, despite the drink.

You order another round.

As the bartender pours the drinks, he catches your eye. Your heart skips a beat. With the bolt of unexpected energy transferred over the counter, an image enters your inner vision; the barman's clothes shimmer and become a panther pelt; his hair becomes wild and darkly lustrous, full of ivy; his countenance gleams with youthful mischief and energy. You could swear you saw some of this ambrosial light land in each of the five drinks he is pouring.

A blink later, and he is back to his old, regular self.

Mystified, you return to the table with your various beverages. Your friends are still droning on about something-in-nothing, and you, reclining and wondering what you bothered coming out for, take a sip of your drink.

Hop-ziggety! The liquid froths and fizzes on your tongue in a way it certainly did not before; then, before you know it, it is fizzling its way through your entire body, making you feel as if your veins were running with champagne.

Your friends are beginning to take sips of their own drinks, and, judging from their instantaneous smiles and lively faces, are experiencing something similar to you. Everyone looks into their glass, then sheepishly around, not wishing to comment lest they are simply imagining it. Still, the drinks go down very swiftly, and as the conversation develops onto a more interesting and animated topic, concerning experiences of ecstasy, someone else gets in another round.

The next drink seems even more infused with effervescence. As you imbibe, you become giggly and inspired. Everyone else is the same. The conversation rapidly deteriorates from a meaningful discussion of personal rhapsody to random hilarity, with everyone carried away by hysterical laughter.

More drinks are brought to the rowdy table. Your last conscious thought is to wonder where the walls have gone.

Now you are in an Arcadian bower, still with the same companions, and still with the drink, but you have developed goat shanks or the form of a nymph (you choose), and your senses are dominated by the dizziness of drink and the pulsating, compelling music issuing from a lyre-bearing golden being of light, in conjunction with the fine reed-notes steeping from a horned goat-man you realize is Pan. Apollo and Pan play together for the entertainment of the throng, while you and your friends compulsively imbibe.

Imagine yourself very strongly into this situation. Imagine your crown chakra being drenched in dazzling light as you take more and more from your chalice. The bartender is here too, dressed as you envisaged him earlier, in a spotted pelt, smooth skinned and wild of gesture. He flashes his palms at you, and a brilliant light and motion carries you out of the top of your head.

Out here, all is boundless, united by the life-force, with no perimeters, no definitions of difference. You feel the network of life all around you, and your body like a lightbulb, at present switched on and shining brightly, but it is a concentration of matter which you realize is only temporarily connected.

Fly around and see what you experience when driven by pleasure. Let the thought of revelry fuel you, the taste of the alcohol still on your tongue, the celestial fuzziness still in your veins. Use all of your energy to perceive the beauty of a flower, the complexities of a melody, the blueness of the sky. Feel how life dances through and with us, and let your mind go.

Return to your normal state when the stream of imagery has played itself out.

VISUALIZATION FOR RELEASING EMOTION VERBALLY OR ARTISTICALLY

How many times have you been told you "never talk"—at least, about emotional issues? For men especially, lack of communication is a disease. This can become literal, as nothing is so well placed to create psychosomatic problems as suppressed emotion.

However, for some, the idea of sharing feelings seems soppy and inappropriate. Many men see it as irrelevant, and would rather concentrate on objective facts. When their relationships break down around them, they wonder why.

Dionysus expresses the antithesis of this inhibited stance. He is all free-flowing emotion, expression, and pleasure. He knows no taboos, and though he is far from a sensitive, caring, sharing god, he can lead the way to such a condition. Dionysus releases the soul curtailed by convention and habit. He transforms compressed emotions into the seeds of creativity.

This is a simple visualization which employs in part the technique known as "assumption of godforms." This involves relating to, envisaging and then "becoming" the god. Obviously this can be very inadvisable in its extreme forms, and this exercise is a watered-down version. A proper dose of Dionysiac wine would send anyone reeling. The idea here is to adopt enough of the god's qualities to facilitate a state of freedom rather than frenzy. It was through self-discipline and the tutoring of Silenus that the mad, inebriated Dionysus became sober enough to be admitted into the divine realms of Olympus.

Imagine yourself naked but for a pelt loincloth and shoots of ivy in your hair. You are young, beautiful, and fancy-free.

Around you, extending to about seven inches from your skin, is a divine aura. It is bright, clear yellowy-white, with occasional currents of emerald green. It fills you with vigor and rejuvenates your every sense.

You are standing knee-deep in grapes. These are the fruits of your past experiences; each one reminiscent of a different scenario, emotion, or event. Some are green, reminding you of learning processes; others are shriveled, reflecting your more painful moments, and others are dark and ripe, succulent memories you savor.

It seems as if your entire life to date is gathered in this vat—for now you notice that you are standing in one. The walls are oak, you decide, on reflection. It is, of course, down to you in your Dionysiac persona to compress, distill, and ferment your past into a potion that could carry your soul toward the divine.

So, trample your past. As you do so, bursting the skins of old experiences, mingling them together, feel yourself being thrust still further into the referents and sensations of ever-youthful Dionysus, the barriers which stand between you and communication (even if you prefer it that way) splitting like the grape skins.

Just as the juices of the different grapes are being freed and creating new combinations, determine to release the different elements of your past and allow them to inspire you with new thoughts and perceptions. You are not trampling them merely to break the bonds and force them to merge, but also in the hope of eliciting something sweet and new from the combination. The "inebriation" you get from this should inspire you to new creative and communicative heights.

Tread the wine for as long as you feel is relevant. When you are thigh-deep in the fluid of your past, mix it, leave the vat, and mentally cover it over. Send a ray of light from your third eye, hidden somewhere beneath your dark, wild mane of curling hair, and see it stimulating the ferment-ing process.

When the latter is complete—one great thing about visualizations is the lack of time restriction—you may imbibe some of the homegrown wine. Or all of it. Visualize yourself partaking of the processed results of your past actions, and feel the liberation that comes from having turned them into a source of elevation rather than confinement.

You could drink some real wine at this point and envisage your past absorbed into it. When you feel suitably inebriated, it is time to get out the word processor, guitar, or paintbrush. Alternately, you could prove whoever it was who accused you of "never speaking" to be wrong, by surprising them which a bout of emotional articulation.

Even if you are required to be Apolline during the day, you can be Dionysiac at night. This is a common pattern, and one that often saves the sanity of those who use it. As mentioned above, a little madness is often necessary. There is as much spiritual insanity in the "civic" as in the "uncivilized." As with all things, particularly occult and psychological, a balance between extremes is the most desirable and progressive state.

Mundane Archetypes

Dionysus is the classic rock musician, with all the entailing indulgences in drugs, drink, and women. Jim Morrison was renowned for his empathy with the Dionysus archetype and others who drove themselves to the extreme for the sake of pleasure also fit the bill—Jimi Hendrix and Michael Hutchence, for example. There were many tragedies in the 1960s, one of Dionysus' eras (along with the end of the Roman Empire), a time in which communion with God through the divine inebriation of drugs and meditation overtook the Apolline 1950s, in which information was logically communicated and received, rather than intuitively perceived.

Dionysus has a great deal of charisma, and his attitude is distinctly cavalier. He flouts convention and deliberately provokes a reaction in others. He challenges accepted standards and presents a spirited alternative, usually involving poetry, Epicurean/Hedonistic philosophy, a bit of melancholy and nostalgia for innocence lost, and definitely music.

His mundane archetype can, however, be full of bullshit, which he is happy to expound anyway because he believes that if anyone is stupid enough to listen to it, they deserve what they get. There is a hard center to this soft-skinned, longhaired youth, and a relentless selfishness which others find extremely attractive. The danger is that he is often mistaken for a guru, when really he is just a vivacious and talented pleasure-seeker.

The Dionysus-character is only interested in religion in as far as it is captivating and fun. His attention span is short and he leaps from one project to the next, often failing to complete any of them. He is artistic, and at least one of him is found on every arts-degree course and in many bands. Those who work with him always find their own ideas enhanced in his effervescent presence. He seeks adrenaline rushes perpetually, the pursuit of which leads him to travel, bungee-jump, take the scariest rides at the fair, and challenge his fear threshold at every opportunity.

The Dionysiac spirit never lives in its entirety beyond thirty-five; if he manages it physically, he transforms into another archetype such as Hermes, Zeus (paternity can do this to him), or, at worst, Ra.

TAROT CARDS

The Fool, The Devil

Conclusion

There is possibly an even greater diversity of male gods in the cosmos than there is female; at least, of which we are commonly aware. In this book alone we have witnessed the loving kindness of Krishna and the arrogant, unyielding power of Zeus; the esoteric mysteries of Thoth and the pragmatism of Ganesh.

Invoke the Gods and *Invoke the Goddess* present just thirty of the deities we can work with, both psychologically and spiritually, to attain specific ends. The possibilities for work with godforms are, however, innumerable. Each arcane expression of human belief has his or her place in the group and individual psyche, and each is a valid magickal and psychological tool. As William Blake put it, "Everything Possible to be Believ'd is an Image of Truth."

The exercises in these books are examples. The descriptions and histories are factually accurate, allowing the reader to build a precise picture of each deity.

However, the effects are of course interpretative. Nothing beats individual experience, in any scenario, and I hope that *Invoke the Gods* and *Invoke the Goddess* will furnish the reader with ideas and inspiration for powerful workings of their own device.

Kala Trobe
London
December 2000

GLOSSARY

Ajna: Third Eye. This term usually refers to the pineal/pituitary chakra between the brows.

Ascetic: see **Renunciant**

Astral Body: In Western terms, the third body (after the physical and subtle), relating to emotion, dreams, and creative inspiration. It is usually the vehicle for astral travel.

Aura: The energy which emanates from and surrounds an object, such as the human body. The human aura reflects the spiritual, mental, and physical well-being of a person, and has several layers, visible to the psychic eye. Plants and trees have less complex auras. Inanimate objects such as stones or jewelry can absorb the aura of their owners, and retain it for centuries. There are also auras created by particular circumstances (such as a ceremony), and group auras. To some extent, the aura is the sum of all of the parts of a person, object, or group. On a big scale, countries have auras, as do planets.

Binah: Sephirah (sphere) on the Qabalistic Tree of Life (see **Qabalah**) at the top of the Pillar of Severity. Binah represents form, female energy and capacity, and the qualities of synthesis and understanding. It is the counterpart of dynamic **Chokmah.**

Caduceus: A winged staff entwined about by two serpents, which cross on the staff at four points, representing the elements. The Caduceus is Mercurial in origin and refers to the concomitant qualities. As well as indicating communicative intelligence, the Caduceus represents balance of energies both microcosmic and macrocosmic. It is thus related to the healing aspect of Hermes.

Causal Body: The finest of the body sheaths, relating to the highest principles of individual and cosmic existence.

Chakra: Focal points on the body, variously described as wheels, whirlpools, and discs of light, these centers distribute life-energy throughout the psycho-spiritual and physical systems. They are used in many yogic techniques, and can be utilized in visualization and magick as keys to specific traits and aspects of the self, as well as to engender particular energy levels. The seven major chakras, which run down the spine from the top of the head, are the Crown, the Ajna or Third Eye, the Throat, the Heart, the Solar Plexus, the Intestinal, and finally the Base or Root chakra, which abides, as its name suggests, at the base of the spine.

Chesed: On the Tree of Life in the **Qabalah**, the central sphere on the Pillar of Mercy, representative of this quality.

Chokmah: Meaning "wisdom," this sephirah is placed at the top of the Pillar of Mercy on the Qabalistic Tree of Life. It is masculine and dynamic, and counterbalances the feminine potency of **Binah**.

Crown: Refers to the **chakra** at the top of the skull, represented by the thousand-petalled lotus of meditative symbolism.

Dharma: The Sanskrit name for the principle of cosmic order. The code of conduct of the individual that safeguards integrity and ensures longevity of the soul. Virtue and the upholding of sacred law. In nature, the balance and sustenance of the universe.

Dighambara (sky-clad): The state of being physically naked, but clad in spiritual grace. Devotees of Siva and Kali are particularly inclined to it. Some Wiccans also practice ritual nudity, with the intent of becoming more "at one with nature." In Hinduism, *dighambara* is used to dispel all earthly ties and to represent total trust in and attention to God.

Geburah: In **Qabalah**, the central sephirah of the Pillar of Severity, representing the breaking-down processes of the cosmos.

Hod: The lowest sphere of the Pillar of Severity of the **Qabalah**, representing Mercurial properties such as intellectual debate and communication of ideas. Hod is a sephirah in which form is emphasized.

Kali Yuga: According to Hindu doctrine, the present and most pernicious of four great Ages of Man, which will be terminated by the coming of the Kalki Avatar, the final incarnation of Vishnu. In the meantime, we are advised that the chanting of mantras will liberate us from the bonds of this materialistic aeon. The Maha Mantra of Krishna is purported to be particularly effective in this context.

Karma: Essentially, the principle that what goes around, comes around. The law of cause and effect, often applicable from one life to the next and influencing the conditions of one's birth and lateral circumstances. This is not so much as a punishment, as is sometimes implied, but in order to bring about the scenario necessary for reparation and development. It is believed by some that actions are magnified threefold, so that a good action will bring triple recompense and a cruel or selfish one will bring three times as much pain to its perpetrator.

Kether: The sephirah at the crown of the Tree of Life, signifying the nearest proximity to God.

Malkuth: The lowest sephirah on the Tree of Life, crossing over into the earth plane.

Netzach: The lowest sphere on the Pillar of Mercy, the natural, energetic counterpart to dogmatic Hod. While Hod represents the glory of the intellect, Netzach signifies the beauty and final victory of love.

Pythia: A priestess of Apollo, oracular in intent.

Qabalah: The ancient Jewish mystical system of Kabbalah as employed by the Western Mystery Tradition. This highly eclectic system seeks to unify symbols and experiences by attributing them to one of ten states of being (the sephiroth) or twenty-two states of becoming (the paths). These attributes are placed in diagrammatic form upon the

Tree of Life. This consists of a Pillar of Severity, a Middle Pillar of Equilibrium, and a Pillar of Mercy. At its crown sits **Kether**, representing the nearest conceivable proximity to the Cosmic Intelligence, while its root is signified by **Malkuth**, which overlaps with the material plane of our mundane existence. Qabalah is a practical philosophy as well as a mystical technique.

Renunciant (Ascetic): One who gives up fleshly pleasures and ambitions in order to concentrate on the search for God. In India, this often means possessing nothing but a begging bowl and perhaps a strip of cloth.

Sadhu: A holy man in Hinduism, often similar to the renunciant above. The Sadhu is a seeker of God, sometimes a sage, always a yogi.

Shakti: The female energy of the *primum mobile;* the feminine side of God. Usually referred to with reference to the Siva, or masculine contingent of the psyche/cosmos.

Siddhi powers: Tricks, usually of a lower psychic nature, which are facilitated by the side effect of particular types of meditation and yogic practice. Sai Baba's manifestation of holy ash is one example; the ability of some masters to appear in two places at once is another.

Tiphareth: The sephirah central to the Tree of Life; a mystical energy-nucleus, signifying balance, harmony, and spiritual beauty.

Udjat (Uatchat): The Eye of Horus, central to Egyptian esoteric symbolism. The Udjat is all-seeing, both externally and internally; a perpetual reminder of the need for integrity on all levels, of the transience of the mortal state and the eventual assessment of one's life.

Uraeus: A serpent symbol, usually found at the center of a headdress. It represented earthly power, particularly regal. Pharaohs wore it to signify this and their connection with Ra and Horus, to whom the uraeus was particularly relevant.

Yesod: The Astral sphere on the Tree of Life, above **Malkuth** and below **Tiphareth** on the Middle Pillar. This is the center of dreams, the subconscious and low-level magick.

BIBLIOGRAPHY

Aeschylus. *The Oresteian Trilogy.* (trans. Philip Vellacott.) Middlesex, England: Penguin Books Ltd., 1956.

Atchity, Kenneth J. *The Classical Greek Reader.* New York, N.Y.: Henry Holt, 1996.

Bailey, Alice A. *The Unfinished Autobiography.* London, England: Lucis Publishing Trust, 1994.

———. *The Seven Rays of Life.* London, England: Lucis Publishing Trust, 1995.

Barrett, Clive. *The Egyptian Gods and Goddesses.* London, England: Diamond Books, 1996.

Blake, William. *A Selection of Poems and Letters.* Middlesex, England: Penguin Books Ltd., 1976.

Budge, Sir A. E. Wallis. *Books on Egypt and Chaldea*. London, England: Routledge & Kegan Paul Ltd., 1956.

———. *The Egyptian Heaven and Hell*. Chicago, Ill., USA: Open Court Publishing Company, 1997.

Carriere, Jean-Claude. *The Mahabharata*. (trans. Peter Brook.) London, England: Methuen, 1987.

Euripides. *The Bacchae and Other Plays*. (trans. Philip Vellacott.) Middlesex, England: Penguin Books Ltd., 1974.

———. *Medea/Hecabe/Electra/Heracles*. (trans. Philip Vellacott.) Middlesex, England: Penguin Books Ltd., 1974.

Evelyn-White, Hugh G. (trans.). *Hesiod, Homeric Hymns, Epic Cycle, Homerica*. Harvard University Press, London, England: Loeb Classic, 1998.

Fortune, Dion. *The Goat-Foot God*. London, England: Star Books, 1976.

———. *Moon Magic*. London, England: Society of the Inner Light, 1995.

———. *The Sea Priestess*. Northamptonshire, England: Aquarian Press, 1989.

Goodman, Frederick. *Magic Symbols*. London, England: Brian Todd Publishing House, 1989.

Hammond, N. G. L., and H. H. Scullard. *The Oxford Classical Dictionary*. Oxford, England: OUP Clarendon Press, 1989.

Handelman, Don, and David Shulman. *God Inside Out: Siva's Game of Dice*. New York, N.Y.: Oxford University Press, 1997.

Harshananda, Swami. *Hindu Gods and Goddesses*. Madras, India: Ramakrishna Math, 1987.

Homer. *The Iliad*. (trans. Robert Fitzgerald.) Oxford, England: World's Classics, Oxford University Press, 1988.

———. *The Odyssey*. (trans. E. V. Rieu.) Middlesex, England: Penguin Books Ltd., 1977.

Hughes, Ted. *Tales from Ovid*. London, England: Faber and Faber Limited, 1997.

Hyde, Lewis. *Trickster Makes This World*. New York, N.Y.: Farrar, Straus and Giroux, 1998.

Ikram, Salima and Aidan Dodson. *The Mummy in Ancient Egypt*. London, England: Thames and Hudson Ltd., 1998.

Ions, Veronica. *Egyptian Mythology*. Middlesex, England: Hamlyn Publishing Group Ltd., 1968.

Larousse. (ed. Robert Graves.) *Larousse Encyclopaedia of Mythology*. London, England: Paul Hamlyn, 1964.

Lloyd-Jones, Sir Hugh. *The Justice of Zeus*. Los Angeles, Calif.: University of California Press, 1983.

Otto, Walter F. *The Homeric Gods*. London, England: Thames and Hudson Ltd., 1979.

Pai, Anant (ed.). *Hanuman*. Mumbai, India: India Book House Limited, 1999.

———. (ed.). *Krishna*. Mumbai, India: India Book House Limited, 1999.

Plutarch. *Isis and Osiris*. (Moralia, Volume V). London, England: Loeb Editions, 1987.

Prabhupada, Swami A. C. Bhaktivedanta. *Bhagavad-Gita As It Is*. Los Angeles, Calif.: Bhaktivedanta Book Trust, 1986.

————. *The Perfection of Yoga*. North South Wales, Australia: Bhaktivedanta Book Trust, 1984.

Prabhavananda, Swami, and Christopher Isherwood (trans.). *Bhagavad-Gita, Song of God*. Madras, India: Sri Ramakrishna Math, undated.

Ramanujan, A. K. *Speaking of Siva*. Middlesex, England: Penguin Books Ltd., 1987.

Regardie, Israel. *A Garden of Pomegranates*. London, England: Rider & Company, 1932.

Rose, H. J. *A Handbook of Greek Mythology*. London, England: Routledge, 1991.

Sharman-Burke, Juliet. *The Mythic Tarot Workbook*. London, England: Rider, 1989.

Skelton, Robin. *Spellcraft: A Manual of Verbal Magic*. London, England: Routledge & Kegan Paul, 1978.

Sophocles. *The Theban Plays*. (trans. E. F. Watling.) Middlesex, England: Penguin Books Ltd., 1947.

Spence, Lewis. *Egypt: Myths and Legends*. London, England: Senate, 1994.

Trevelyan, Sir George. *A Vision of the Aquarian Age*. Bath, England: Gateway Books, 1977.

Trobe, Kala. *Invoke the Goddess: Visualizations of Hindu, Greek and Egyptian Deities*. St. Paul, Minn., USA: Llewellyn Publications, 2000.

Vishnu-Devananda, Swami. *Meditations and Mantras*. New York, N.Y.: OM Lotus Publishing Company, 1995.

Vivekananda, Swami. *Hanuman Chalisa*. Madras, India: Sri Ramakrishna Math, undated.

Waterstone, Richard. *India*. London, England: Duncan Baird Publishers, Macmillan, 1995.

Watterson, Barbara. *Gods of Ancient Egypt*. Gloucestershire, England: Sutton Publishing Limited, 1996.

West, M. L. *Ancient Greek Music*. Oxford, England: OUP, Clarendon Press, 1992.

Yogananda, Paramahansa. *Autobiography of a Yogi*. Los Angeles, Calif.: Self-Realization Fellowship, 1990.

Zaehner, R. C. *Hindu Scriptures*. London, England: Everyman's Library, David Campbell Publishers Ltd., 1992.

Index

REACH FOR THE MOON

Llewellyn publishes hundreds of books on your favorite subjects!
To get these exciting books, including the ones on the following pages,
check your local bookstore or order them directly from Llewellyn.

Order by Phone
- Call toll-free within the U.S. and Canada, 1-800-THE MOON
- In Minnesota, call (651) 291-1970
- We accept VISA, MasterCard, and American Express

Order by Mail
- Send the full price of your order (MN residents add 7% sales tax) in U.S. funds, plus postage & handling to:

  Llewellyn Worldwide
  P.O. Box 64383, Dept. 0-7387-0096-7
  St. Paul, MN 55164–0383, U.S.A.

Postage & Handling
- **Standard** (U.S., Mexico, & Canada)

If your order is:
  $20.00 or under, add $5.00
  $20.01–$100.00, add $6.00
  Over $100, shipping is free
(Continental U.S. orders ship UPS. AK, HI, PR, & P.O. Boxes ship USPS 1st class. Mex. & Can. ship PMB.)

- **Second Day Air** (Continental U.S. only): $10.00 for one book + $1.00 per each additional book
- **Express** (AK, HI, & PR only) [Not available for P.O. Box delivery. For street address delivery only.]: $15.00 for one book + $1.00 per each additional book
- **International Surface Mail:** Add $1.00 per item
- **International Airmail:** Books—Add the retail price of each item; Non-book items—Add $5.00 per item

Please allow 4–6 weeks for delivery on all orders.
Postage and handling rates subject to change.

Discounts
We offer a 20% discount to group leaders or agents. You must order a minimum of 5 copies of the same book to get our special quantity price.

Free Catalog
Get a free copy of our color catalog, *New Worlds of Mind and Spirit*. Subscribe for just $10.00 in the United States and Canada ($30.00 overseas, airmail). Many bookstores carry *New Worlds*—ask for it!

Visit our website at www.llewellyn.com for more information.

Invoke the Goddess
Visualizations of Hindu, Greek & Egyptian Deities

KALA TROBE

Appeal to the Hindu goddess Sarasvati to help you ace an exam. Find your ideal long-term partner through Isis. Invoke Artemis for strength and confidence in athletics.

Invoke the Goddess shows you how to link with the specific archetypal energies of fifteen different goddess through simple exercises and visualizations. This magickal workbook allows anyone, no matter how limited or developed her occult prowess, into a direct encounter with a powerful archetypal deity whose symbols and presence will make a profound impression on the subconscious.

Whether you want to accomplish a specific goal or integrate the murkier areas of your psyche, this book will lead you step by step through your inner journeys. The author explains different ways of carrying out the exercises, how to take ritual baths with solarized water, and preparation through chakra work, diet, and exercise.

1-56718-431-6, 240 pp., 7 ¹/₂ x 9 ¹/₈, illus.   **$14.95**

Magic of Qabalah
Visions of the Tree of Life

KALA TROBE

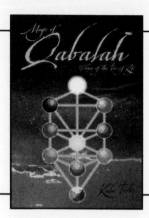

This introduction to the Golden Dawn system of Qabalah covers the usual ground in an unusual way. It uses creative visualizations and analysis of mythologies and tarot symbolism to bring the reader into a direct, personal experience of this universal system. Use the exercises for specific purposes as diverse as physical/spiritual courage (Geburah), integration (Binah), and magickal foundation building (Malkuth).

The introduction provides a condensed history of the Qabalah, along with a quick trip up the Tree of Life to familiarize the novice with the system, plus information on its metaphysical context and use of Tarot attributions.

Ten chapters follow, one for each Sephirah, containing an exploration of its traits and contemporary application, a brief description of the Path by which one might mentally arrive at the desired destination, and information on the God names, Angels, and symbols. Each chapter culminates in a guided creative visualization.

- Interact on a more personal level with the system of the Qabalah
- Make this spiritual system a living, growing reality for your life
- Make contact with the energies of each Sephirah through guided visualizations
- Deepen your understanding through "A Qabalistic Tale," an allegorical story based on Tree of Life symbolism

0-7387-0002-9, 336 pp., 6 x 9 $14.95

To order, call 1-800-THE MOON
Prices subject to change without notice

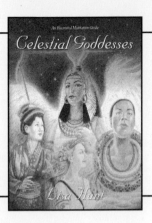

Celestial Goddesses
An Illustrated Meditation Guide

LISA HUNT

Original art depicts twenty goddesses in all their heavenly beauty. They personify the heavens, and they gave birth to the sun, the moon, and the stars. They had the power to create and to restore lives. Now you, too, can nurture and celebrate the feminine divine with the help of *Celestial Goddesses*.

Visualize your own spiritual journey with the aid of twenty original, full-color goddess paintings. From Amaterasu (Japan), whose brother's jealous rampage helped her realize her true beauty, to the creation myth of Mawu (West Africa), each image is accompanied by a description of the symbolism and a guided meditation.

- Hardcover with full-color interior
- The author/artist is the illustrator of Llewellyn's *Shapeshifter Tarot* and *The Celtic Dragon Tarot*
- Goddesses representing twenty different cultures will appeal to readers from various backgrounds
- Each goddess has a poignant story that invites you to relate to her in a very personal way
- A wonderful addition to New Age, fantasy, astrology, and astronomy book collections
- Can be used on many different levels: as an art collection, as an overview of ancient celestial goddess worship, and as a meditative guide

0-7387-0118-1, 144 pp., 8 x 10, full-color interior, hardcover **$24.95**

To order, call 1-800-THE MOON
Prices subject to change without notice

Goddess Meditations

BARBARA ARDINGER, PH.D.
Foreword by
Patricia Monaghan

Bring the presence of the Goddess into your daily spiritual practice with *Goddess Meditations*, a book of seventy-three unique guided meditations created for women and men who want to find a place of centeredness and serenity in their lives, both alone and in groups, either in rituals or informally.

Call on a Hestia for a house blessing . . . the White Buffalo Calf Woman for help in learning from your mistakes . . . Aphrodite for love and pleasure . . . Kuan Yin for compassion. Although it's directed toward experienced meditators, this book includes guidelines for beginners about breathing, safety, and grounding, as well as instructions for rituals and constructing an altar.

Also featured is the powerful "Goddess Pillar Meditation," based on the Qabalistic Middle Pillar Meditation; nine Great Goddess meditations that address issues such as protection, community, and priestess power; and seven meditations that link goddesses to the chakras.

1-56718-034-5, 256 pp., 7 x 10   **$17.95**

The Mysteries of Isis
Her Worship and Magick

deTraci Regula

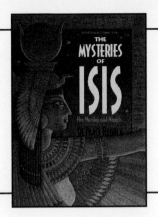

For 6,000 years, Isis has been worshiped as a powerful yet benevolent goddess who loves and cares for those who call on her. Here, for the first time, her secrets and mysteries are revealed in an easy-to-understand form so you can bring the power of this great and glorious goddess into your life.

Mysteries of Isis is filled with practical information on the modern practice of Isis' worship. Other books about Isis treat her as an entirely Egyptian goddess, but this book reveals that she is a universal goddess with many faces, who has been present in all places and in all times. Simple yet effective rituals and exercises will show you how to forge your unique personal alliance with Isis: prepare for initiation into her four key mysteries, divine the future using the Sacred Scarabs, perform purification and healing rites, celebrate her holy days, travel to your own inner temple, cast love spells, create your own tools and amulets, and much more. Take Isis as your personal goddess and your worship and connection with the divine will be immeasurably enriched.

1-56178-560-6, 320 pp., 7 x 10, illus.   **$19.95**

Wiccan Warrior

Walking a Spiritual Path in a Sometimes Hostile World

KERR CUHULAIN

"Being a warrior is not about fighting. It's about freeing yourself of limitations so that you can be truly creative and effective in life." In the current Wiccan community, many archetypes present themselves: Maidens, Mothers, Crones, Healers, Magicians—but rarely Warriors. *Wiccan Warrior* is the first book to show the average Pagan how to access the Warrior archetype within. It demonstrates how to follow a path that is essentially the Wiccan Rede in action: "An it harm none, do what thou wilt."

Written by a Wiccan police officer and martial artist, *Wiccan Warrior* combines personal insights and real-life anecdotes with ritual, magick, energy work, meditation, self-examination, and self-discipline. It is about taking responsibility for your actions, knowing that a true Warrior wins most of his battles with his head, not his hands.

1-56718-252-6, 216 pp., 6 x 9 $12.95

To order, call 1-800-THE MOON
Prices subject to change without notice

The Tree of Life
An Illustrated Study in Magic

ISRAEL REGARDIE
Edited and annotated
by Chic Cicero and Sandra Tabatha Cicero

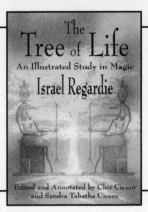

In 1932, when magic was a "forbidden subject," Israel Regardie wrote *The Tree of Life* at the age of 24. He believed that magic was a precise scientific discipline as well as a highly spiritual way of life, and he took on the enormous task of making it accessible to a wide audience of eager spiritual seekers. The result was The Tree of Life, which adroitly presents a massive amount of diverse material in a remarkably unified whole.

From the day it was first published, this book has remained in high demand by ceremonial magicians for its skillful combination of ancient wisdom and modern magical experience. It was Regardie's primary desire to point out the principles of magic that cut across all boundaries of time, religion, and culture—those fundamental principles common to all magic, regardless of any specific tradition or spiritual path.

1-56718-132-5, 552 pp., 6 x 9, 177 illus., full-color, 4-pp. insert $19.95